The Rational Software Engineer

Strategies for a Fulfilling Career in Tech

Mykyta Chernenko

Apress®

The Rational Software Engineer: Strategies for a Fulfilling Career in Tech

Mykyta Chernenko
Oslo, Norway

ISBN-13 (pbk): 978-1-4842-9794-0   ISBN-13 (electronic): 978-1-4842-9795-7
https://doi.org/10.1007/978-1-4842-9795-7

Managing Director, Apress Media LLC: Welmoed Spahr
Acquisitions Editor: Susan McDermott
Development Editor: Laura Berendson
Project Manager: Jessica Vakili

Distributed to the book trade worldwide by Springer Science+Business Media New York, 1 NY PLaza, New York, NY 10004. Phone 1-800-SPRINGER, fax (201) 348-4505, e-mail orders-ny@ springer-sbm.com, or visit www.springeronline.com. Apress Media, LLC is a California LLC and the sole member (owner) is Springer Science + Business Media Finance Inc (SSBM Finance Inc). SSBM Finance Inc is a **Delaware** corporation.

For information on translations, please e-mail booktranslations@springernature.com; for reprint, paperback, or audio rights, please e-mail bookpermissions@springernature.com.

Apress titles may be purchased in bulk for academic, corporate, or promotional use. eBook versions and licenses are also available for most titles. For more information, reference our Print and eBook Bulk Sales web page at http://www.apress.com/bulk-sales.

Any source code or other supplementary material referenced by the author in this book is available to readers on the Github repository: https://github.com/Apress/The-Rational-Software-Engineer. For more detailed information, please visit https://www.apress.com/gp/services/source-code.

Paper in this product is recyclable

Table of Contents

About the Author

Mykyta Chernenko, originally from Kharkiv, Ukraine, now resides in Oslo, Norway. Beginning with back end with Python, Mykyta soon expanded his toolkit to include fullstack development and diverse languages like Go, Kotlin, and TypeScript. Beyond his main technical focus, Mykyta has experience in DevOps, data engineering, and product management.

Throughout his professional journey, Mykyta has been a part of various intriguing projects through his experience in product, outsourcing, and consultancy companies. He contributed to the Azure integration of Nutanix's cluster discovery project and played a central technical role at Factmata, taking over the engineering and infrastructure. He further continued to work in product teams at both Mercell as a tech lead and as a senior software engineer at Arundo Analytics.

Apart from his project contributions, Mykyta has shown a strong passion for teaching and sharing his experience. He has taken on mentoring roles throughout his career, guiding and supporting over 20 professionals in the field, and expressed himself through his blog, "The Rational Software Engineer," on Hackernoon.

Understanding that software engineering is driven by people and their thinking, Mykyta consistently tries to broaden his horizons in the psychology and neurobiology realm through books and courses.

Mykyta is a cofounder of Nemlys—a promising tech startup dedicated to helping couples improve their communication through personalized AI questions for their dates.

Acknowledgments

This book has been an amazing journey for me, and I'm very happy to finish something that I think can benefit other fellow software engineers. But this journey would have been much worse without all the tremendous support and help I got from others.

First of all, I want to say thank you to my wife, who managed to bear with me through the process, which included me constantly rattling about the book, reviews of the book, and providing me with advice. You helped me and treasured my concentration when I was in the flow, and you also motivated me when I went through more challenging days. And most important, you gave me the confidence that I can accomplish such a big task in the first place.

The story of the book started much earlier than when I decided that it was going to become a full-blown book. Initially, the idea was to write a series of articles, and a lot of my friends helped me with that process. Back then, writing was much more of a novel and exciting journey for me, but it also meant that there was a lot of work put into the review of my drafts and providing me with helpful insights. So I'm really grateful to all of my friends, who helped to review the articles at that time and also book chapters later on. I want to give special recognition to Maksym Bekuzarov, who reviewed most of my initial articles, gave me rough but very actionable criticism, and put the idea that something great can come from the idea, and to Artem Korchunov, who was the first reviewer of most of my chapters and provided me with insightful feedback.

Last, but definitely not least, is my official team who made the book possible. I'm grateful to Apress and its members including Jessica Vakili, Susan McDermott, and Laura C. Berendson for a good navigating with

ACKNOWLEDGMENTS

the process and a smooth journey. I also want to say special thanks to my
official reviewer, Brad Dolin, who gave me a lot of new perspectives on
what I wrote and greatly complemented what I wrote in the spheres of
physiology, studies, and management.

Introduction

Software engineers are often seen as very smart professionals, and there's a good reason for that. Our job is all about solving problems. We take big, complicated tasks and break them down into smaller, more manageable pieces. Then we use code to create solutions. This requires a clear understanding of the problem, a lot of logical thinking, and attention to detail.

Becoming a software engineer is not a small feat either. The path to our occupation demands rigorous education, intensive training, and a relentless pursuit of knowledge. We can spend years studying complex mathematical theories, intricate algorithms, and multiple programming languages. But formal education is just the tip of the iceberg. Breaking into the field often requires countless hours of hands-on practice, building projects, debugging errors, and self-teaching new technologies and tools. The high barrier to entry ensures that those who do become software engineers have demonstrated not only academic aptitude but also determination, adaptability, and creativity.

On top of our technical skills, we often develop a good sense of resilience. Debugging, for example, is a significant part of our job. We may spend hours or even days trying to find a tiny error in our code that's causing a big problem. This process can be frustrating, but it teaches patience, persistence, and a methodical approach to problem-solving. Every bug we resolve, every challenge we face and overcome, only sharpens our analytical skills. It's like a mental gym where we constantly exercise and grow our cognitive muscles. And the tech world also changes fast. New tools, languages, and techniques come up all the time. Software engineers have to keep learning and adapting, or they'll get left behind.

So there is no doubt that software engineers are smart. But with everything mentioned earlier, with all the proven track record of high intelligence, there is still a big portion of software engineers who are not particularly happy about their job and who don't seem like a good example of what a happy and fulfilled software engineer is. And at some point, I realized that I was affected by that as well. As nice as it was with all of the friendly environment and great perks, I noticed that my passion, satisfaction, and curiosity were decreasing. My state was not terrible, but far from calling it happy and satisfied. And the worst of it seemed to be that it got a little worse with every year. It didn't bring as much joy to code as it used to do, I started caring less, and I became less interested and curious. I clearly had a looming problem, and I needed to find solutions.

I understood that there was clearly something missing—something that goes beyond pure cognitive abilities and common knowledge I had, something that would help me to foster a high level of passion and satisfaction with what I did. So I began to search for answers, reading a lot of material trying to understand what the best and proven ways to regain the levels of my career happiness are and experimenting with myself to find out what helps me personally.

And the main topics I discovered are exactly what we're going to talk about in this book: Passion, Mindset, and Learning. Passion will cover topics around satisfaction, burnout, organizing your time, and making career changes. Mindset will describe helpful attitudes to lifelong learning, collaboration, health, and values, while the Learning part goes deep into what to learn and how to do it in the most efficient way both on your own and from others.

Passion, Mindset, and Learning are the three pillars we are going to focus on to not only succeed in the field but also truly enjoy the process. When you read all of this, a thought can get into your head, "This sounds suspiciously fluffy." And I understand you here; all of the topics I outlined can be covered in a very fluffy and abstract manner. But this is not the approach I've taken here. This book is going to be very information- and protocol-dense, as this was my idea from the start to make the book short, to the point, and actionable. When you finish the book, you will be equipped with a wide range of specific tools and techniques that you can exercise to improve your career and make it more enjoyable, meaningful, and less stressful.

There is also a reason why I chose the word "rational" to be in the title of the book. To be rational is not just about being logical; it's a commitment to a certain way of approaching problems and making decisions. It means to heavily rely on solid logic, ensuring that conclusions stem from sound reasoning rather than whims or biases. It's about turning to scientific methods, which prioritize evidence and empirical data over mere speculation. Being rational also signifies the wisdom to choose the best tool available for a job, recognizing that every situation might demand a different approach or technique. And this is the approach we're going to utilize here.

At the same time, I don't want to give you a false image that I'm some kind of a guru who has got enlightened and can teach you everything you need to know. I'm clearly not. Like many of you, I'm a software engineer. While I don't have all the answers, I've dedicated a significant amount of time to learning from reputable sources and brilliant minds on the topics. So what I'm going to do is stick to these sources to provide you with the most relevant scientific knowledge and the best insights in the field. If there are two good opinions with their own pros and cons on a topic, I will try to cover both of the positions impartially. And for the absence of a better source in some cases, I will also include my personal reflections and experience to provide you with a complete picture.

Now, as you've got prepared for what you're going to get from this book, let's start our journey by talking about passion.

PART I

Passion

Most of us spend about 20% of our awake time at work over our lifetime, and this number rises to 30% [1] during our working years. Given we spend so much of our lives at work, it makes sense to do it in a way that brings us joy, right? Unfortunately, many people don't actively work toward improving their job satisfaction, work-life balance, or passion for what they do. These are factors that contribute to our overall happiness in life.

Many say that job satisfaction comes easy in the IT industry, and I agree. There are many attractive aspects, like flat hierarchies common in IT companies, HR departments dedicated to improving your experience, generous fun budgets, numerous perks, and high salaries. With all these benefits in place, why would we need to make any extra effort for job satisfaction?

However, there's a catch. Despite the apparent perks of being a software engineer, not everyone in the field is satisfied. According to research by PayScale [2], only 57% of software engineers said they were either "Extremely Satisfied" or "Fairly Satisfied" with their jobs, while only 29% felt their job had high meaning. You might think that it's impossible to please everyone, and perhaps a 57% satisfaction rate and 29% sense of meaningfulness is the best we can expect.

In fact, when compared to other IT-related roles, software engineers fall behind. For instance, computer and information scientists report a 78% satisfaction rate, and computer hardware engineers report a 53% sense of job meaning. These figures significantly surpass those for software engineers. And to add even more to it, surgeons top the charts, 96% find their job meaningful, and 83% report high job satisfaction.

The good news is that everything mentioned above is within our control. Making sure you are passionate, happy, and striving at work is a skill, and this skill can be learned. By changing our attitudes, using appropriate strategies in different situations, and most importantly, picking the right workplace, we can definitely get there. We are going to cover the following chapters in this part:

Chapter 1, "Job Satisfaction": We'll talk about cultural differences, understand the roots of dissatisfaction, and arm you with strategies to foster team well-being, navigate the "us vs. them" mindset, and understand the principle of "skin in the game."

Chapter 2, "Work Time Organization": Time isn't just about hours; it's about how you use them. I'll challenge myths about working hours, introduce the concept of focused work, and share tools for effective task management, combating procrastination, and ensuring high productivity.

Chapter 3, "There Is No Perfect Project": Shatter the myth of the "perfect project." Here, we will cover effective onboarding, learning from challenging projects, and making informed decisions about when and where to shift your focus.

Chapter 4, "Initiative": Explore ways to proactively contribute, from mentoring to knowledge sharing, and understand the ripple effects of your initiative on your career growth.

Chapter 5, "Burnout": Confront the silent challenge of burnout. We'll illuminate its signs, dissect its causes, and pave a path toward recovery, resilience, and stress management.

Chapter 6, "What to Avoid in the Long Run": Identify and sidestep long-term self-sabotage behaviors. From tackling challenging tasks head-on to navigating toward more sustainable work practices.

Chapter 7, "Career Change": Navigate the minor and major career change with confidence. We will cover reassessing your trajectory, considering managerial roles, or changing specializations altogether.

Chapter 8, "How to Find a Dream Job": Master the nuances of effective job hunting, from CV crafting to acing interviews, and learn to assess potential employers for the perfect fit.

References

[1]   https://revisesociology.com/2016/08/16/percentage-life-work/?utm_content=cmp-true

[2]   www.payscale.com/data-packages/most-and-least-meaningful-jobs

CHAPTER 1

Job Satisfaction

We've seen that being a software engineer is not without its challenges when it comes to achieving job satisfaction. Let's first delve into the universal aspects of job satisfaction before turning our focus onto the unique elements that apply specifically to software engineers and their teams. Additionally, we'll explore ways to enhance these factors and discuss effective strategies for dealing with those aspects that are beyond our control.

Main Aspects of Job Satisfaction

Numerous studies have researched this topic, particularly focusing on the role of salary in job satisfaction. For instance, both the 2014 SAP survey [1] and the 2013 SHRM survey [2] highlighted pay as the primary factor. However, a recent study by the Boston Consulting Group [3], which encompassed over 200,000 people worldwide, shows that employees are putting more emphasis on intrinsic rewards and less on compensation.

In the study, participants from different cultures were asked to select their top five criteria from a list of 26 potential factors. Here are the ten most frequently chosen factors for workplace happiness:

- Appreciation for your work

- Good relationships with colleagues

- Good work-life balance

© Mykyta Chernenko 2023
M. Chernenko, *The Rational Software Engineer*,
https://doi.org/10.1007/978-1-4842-9795-7_1

- Good relationships with superiors

- Company's financial stability

- Learning and career development

- Job security

- Attractive fixed salary

- Interesting job content

- Company values

It's key to understand that this list isn't ranked—it's just a list. Why? Because what matters most can change a lot from one person to another and from one culture to another. For example, in Switzerland, having good coworkers is really important. On the other hand, folks in China care a lot about learning and growing in their careers, while in the Philippines, having a stable job is the top concern.

If you're finding it hard to figure out your top five job happiness factors, here's a tip: think about your work life without one of these things. If you think you'd be okay without it, then maybe it's not so important for you. For example, I've met quite a few people who don't worry much about job security because they like the idea of changing jobs every few years.

However, I believe most of us would agree that these factors form the core of a good and enjoyable work environment. So, our goal should be to find a workplace where most of these elements exist and then work on improving the rest. Later in this book, we'll dive into each criterion in more detail. We'll discuss how to spot them when you're choosing a new job and how to foster them in your current workplace.

Now, let's dig deeper into aspects of job satisfaction that are specific to software engineers.

Software Engineers' Aspects of Job Satisfaction

In another study, more than 1300 developers were asked to assess factors that make them unhappy [4]. The findings were pretty interesting. The two main reasons for unhappiness are being stuck on a technical task and time pressure. We will cover how to deal with time pressure later on, but what can we do about being stuck? There are multiple techniques to be more efficient moving forward when you are stuck:

- **Research and Reference**: Use resources such as StackOverflow, GitHub, or official documentation to see if others have encountered similar problems. AI tools such as ChatGPT can be useful for answering coding questions and even spotting and fixing bugs. I often turn to it first when I have a technical challenge.

- **Take a Break**: Sometimes the solution to a challenging problem comes when you step away from it. Your brain continues to process the problem even when you are not consciously thinking about it.

- **Rubber Duck Debugging**: Try to explain the problem to someone else or even to an inanimate object like a rubber duck. This can help you to see the problem from a new perspective and might lead you to the solution.

- **Simplify the Problem**: Break down the problem into smaller, manageable parts. Solve each part individually and then integrate the solutions.

- **Write Tests**: Writing tests for your code can help to isolate the issue and give you a better understanding of where things are going wrong.

- **Desk Code Review**: Get another pair of eyes on your code. A fellow developer might spot something you've missed or suggest a different approach.

- **Use Debugging Tools**: Step through your code with a debugger. This allows you to examine the state of your program at various stages and can help pinpoint where things are going wrong.

- **Revisit Fundamentals**: Go back to the basics. Ensure that your understanding of the problem and the technologies you're using are correct.

- **Rewrite the Code**: If the code is too complex or convoluted, consider rewriting it. Starting from scratch can sometimes be the quickest way to solve a problem.

- **Learn from Past Mistakes**: Keep track of your coding challenges and how you overcame them. This can be a great resource for solving future problems.

- **Avoid Being the Gatekeeper**: Try to always have somebody whose knowledge overlaps with you on project areas; it's especially great if they are more experienced than you are. This is achieved well with rotating teammates often, so that everybody touches most of the code base, or keeping a code domain overlap table, which ensures that at least two people know one area of the code base.

When being stuck combines with time pressure, it can be a recipe for even greater stress. This is especially true when you're up against a tight deadline and can't seem to figure out a crucial bug. I've experienced this a lot in the past, particularly when I was part of small teams. I didn't know then how to react when my manager asked to add one "small" feature right before a release deadline. Now, I understand that last-minute features are usually not a good idea. They tend to be full of bugs, they often cause the team to work overtime, and most of the time, they can actually be postponed to the next sprint without causing any major issues.

I have a clear example of a last-minute feature that should have been pushed to the next work cycle. Just before a product release, we discovered that our app was incorrectly handling time zones. This was a critical issue since one of the app's main features revolved around a calendar and time booking system. After trying to fix the time zone handling in a few places, it became clear that the problem wasn't a specific bug but rather an overall faulty approach to handling time zones. As a result, I had to approach the management and deliver the "exciting" news right before the release. Although there wouldn't be any immediate impact on users (since the platform didn't have any real users at the time, and to be honest, it never got them), we needed to deliver the project to the client. We were already weeks behind schedule and were losing money on the project due to the delay.

Management was reluctant to spend another week's worth of funds from the company's budget on this issue, so they asked me if it was possible to fix the time zone handling by the end of the day. The hero within me couldn't resist the challenge and proudly declared, "Yes, I can finish it by 6:00 or 7:00 p.m." A voice of reason in my mind was trying to remind me, "You don't understand the system well enough, and changing the time zone mechanism could have unpredicted consequences." But at that moment, the possibility of a boosted ego seemed to be stronger than the voice of caution!

The situation unfolded as one might expect. I managed to change the time zone handling relatively quickly, leaving myself an hour to adjust the tests, many of which I was seeing for the first time. My changes broke around 20 tests, but I was determined not to give up. After two hours, I managed to fix all of them, but a couple of tests were still failing for reasons that didn't seem related to time zones. I was on my own; there was only one other engineer on the team, and she was a junior just like me, who didn't understand the tests well enough to offer any help.

After another hour of fruitless efforts, I haven't managed to resolve the issue. At that time, everyone else in the office was gone except for my manager. I approached my manager, feeling completely defeated, to tell her that I hadn't been able to meet the deadline. I didn't understand why the code was broken, and my head was spinning after six straight hours of coding. To me, this felt like a total disaster. I was worried about disappointing my manager whom I greatly admired and saw as a role model. I expected her to be as disappointed as I was, but to my surprise, she took the news calmly, simply responded with a brief "okay" and left for home. Why? Because it turned out that I was the only person who put the stakes so high.

The client didn't even check the app that day. The management team had already switched to their Friday evening relaxation mode. The only person who thought the time zones were crucial was me, and there was no good reason for it. When I fixed the test issue on Monday, which turned out to be due to incorrect concurrent resource access, nobody even noticed that it was not done on Friday. It would have been entirely fine to move this feature to the next sprint and take that Friday evening off, but my ego and lack of experience led me to make the wrong decision.

Reflecting on how I handle situations where I'm stuck on a task or a bug, now that I work in larger teams with more senior members, I almost always have someone to turn to for help. My network has also expanded over time, so if I can't find support within the team, I usually know someone more experienced whom I can reach out to. Having more personal experience also helps me avoid getting stuck. Last but not least, I try to rotate responsibilities within the project with my team members so that none of us becomes the "gatekeeper" for any part of the project.

Not all of the factors I've mentioned are within our control, such as the seniority of our team members, but it's beneficial to be aware of them and to adopt processes that can reduce the likelihood of getting stuck on a problem and not meeting the deadline.

The third significant issue highlighted in the report is dealing with poor quality code and inadequate coding practices. Code debt is a major contributor to poor code quality. Nobody enjoys writing bad code, but sometimes it's unavoidable. It's crucial to manage the code debt in your project effectively. Here are some ways to do that:

- Conducting code reviews with a focus on code quality

- Allocating 20% of each sprint for refactoring

- Discarding code that's meant to be discarded (as much as you'd like to build on your proof of concept, it's often better not to)

- Seeking help from other teams or external consultants for a fresh perspective on your architecture, design document, or your code in general

These strategies can greatly enhance code quality and, in turn, job satisfaction.

The final aspect we'll discuss in this section is what's essential for maintaining a healthy team dynamic.

Well-Being in a Team

A majority of software engineers work as part of a team. These teams can vary in size, but one thing is certain: it's challenging to enjoy your job if you're part of a dysfunctional team. Google, recognizing the importance of effective team dynamics, conducted a research project called "Aristotle" [5]. They identified five key factors that significantly contribute to team efficiency. Here they are, listed in order of importance:

1. **Psychological Safety**: I feel safe taking risks in a team and fail.

2. **Dependability**: My teammates get things done as they promised.

3. **Structure and Clarity**: I have a clear path of what to do and a clear role.

4. **Meaning**: I find my work meaningful.

5. **Impact**: My work makes an impact.

Team efficiency is a strong indicator of a team's well-being, particularly when we see that the main elements of efficiency are psychological safety, dependability, and clarity. We should aim to nurture our team processes and structures to enhance these three areas.

For instance, we can boost psychological safety by allowing team members to make and learn from mistakes instead of punishing them. There's no need to fear asking "silly" questions or experiencing failure—it happens to everyone. Leaders can set the tone by demonstrating that they too are not infallible and that they can discuss their mistakes openly. This promotes a similar mindset in the team. The worst thing a leader can do for psychological safety is to create a culture of fear. I've found that creativity, initiative, and motivation tend to evaporate in such an environment. Likewise, don't hold back from expressing "silly" ideas. Out of every ten "silly" ideas, there's likely to be at least one good one, making it worth sharing them all.

Psychological safety can quickly vanish in a team plagued by emotionally toxic behaviors. That's why it's important to provide feedback to your peers if a joke comes off as offensive or a comment seems aggressive. It's crucial that everyone feels comfortable defending their personal boundaries and that others respect and adapt to those boundaries. While it can take a lot of courage to speak up at times, doing so is incredibly valuable.

Dependability is about having a team of responsible individuals. Only commit to what you can actually deliver and communicate your progress sooner rather than later. It's better to exceed expectations slightly than to fall short. For example, don't commit to completing a feature in three days if you think it'll take four. It's wiser to estimate five days, so your teammates can trust your estimate and be confident that the task will likely be completed in five days. They'll be pleasantly surprised if you finish in three days and won't be disappointed if it takes five. Another important thing is to stick to your general promises. I find it rare that people say that will do something without the intention to do it, but it's fairly common to forget what you said. This is why note-taking is a very useful thing for the tasks that appear. Write down your promises on the list, and it will be much harder to forget them. Or if a task is a little bit bigger, it is a good habit to add it straight to the tracking system.

In terms of structure and clarity, having a clear product vision and well-defined work roles can greatly help. Each team member should know their responsibilities and the overall goals of the project. I once worked on a team where our product vision was unclear, and it was extremely demotivating. We tried to develop a tool for collaboration on a tender, but not knowing the domain in-depth, what users struggle with, and what their typical jobs were quickly led us to a dead end. We were developing features just for the sake of not sitting without work; we didn't know whether it would bring any value or not. Quickly, we went into lengthy architectural and refactoring discussions to improve some details of features we didn't know the value of. It felt like we were moving aimlessly, not really understanding why we were doing what we were doing. This uncertainty greatly reduced our sense of purpose and impact. Luckily, we soon had a skilled product manager join our team, who conducted user and market research and helped us to align what we were doing with the other teams. After that, there was a significant increase in enthusiasm and motivation among the team members because they finally could answer the big "why."

Another important aspect is to strike a balance when it comes to the "us vs. them" mentality. It's important to foster a sense of camaraderie within a team. You should stand up for your teammates, shield them from external criticism, and portray them positively. Essentially, it's fantastic if your team's dynamic makes you feel as though your teammates are your friends.

However, too much of this mentality can bring problems for a team. If you reach a point where you perceive your team as the "good guys" and other teams or management as your "enemies," it can lead to a damaging cycle of poor cooperation within the company. Aim to avoid such extremes. Yes, your team may feel like your close friends, but your other colleagues in the company should also feel like good buddies. We will also talk more about the cons of the "us vs. them" mentality in the next chapters.

Skin in the Game

The concept of having "skin in the game" has gained popularity largely due to Nassim Taleb who wrote a book on the subject. The idea is that when you have something at risk, be it money or reputation, you're more invested in achieving a goal. I've found that applying this concept at work can make your job far more engaging. When you have "skin in the game," you're personally invested in the success of the company, project, or team. Your work gains personal significance as you see how your actions contribute to overall progress.

But how can you create "skin in the game" when you don't own the company and aren't inherently invested in its success? Here are a few approaches:

- **Take Initiative Risks**: Accept responsibility for important projects that could affect your career if they fail. Assume management roles or become a key engineer in presales rounds. You'll quickly see how your success or failure directly impacts the company, lending your work greater significance.

- **Take Reputational Risks**: For example, invite a friend to join the company or promote the company positively on public platforms. This makes you more committed to ensuring that the company is a good place to work.

- **Get Money Involved**: Buy shares or options in the company. This can be a potent way to create "skin in the game." However, it doesn't mean you have to invest all your savings. The goal is simply to invest enough to make the company's success important to you. This strategy is actually pretty popular in tech companies, who try to provide equity to their employees for this purpose.

It's worth noting that you should only create "skin in the game" for companies you genuinely believe in and feel connected to. For instance, if you know the company culture is demoralizing and you're planning to leave soon, it's not worth promoting them socially or inviting friends to join. Similarly, if you see the company is failing despite your best efforts, it wouldn't be wise to invest in it.

How Do I Find All of These?

Now that we've discussed both general and field-specific satisfaction factors, the crucial question is how to find a work environment where all these elements are present. While it's essential to invest time and energy in improving these aspects within your team and company, it can be difficult, if not near impossible, to build them from scratch. The most pragmatic approach is to join a team that's already functioning well.

Evaluating certain aspects such as the level of appreciation, dependability of your future colleagues, and work-life balance can be tricky and prone to errors when done from outside the company during an interview process. We'll delve into this further when we discuss how to find your dream company.

Since you already have insights into your current company—its security level, the experience of management, and the overall agreeableness of the people—there's less to figure out when considering an internal rotation. If, for any reason, your team lacks a healthy level of emotional safety, start looking for teams within your organization where members seem genuinely happy or where the teams are highly efficient. Chances are, these teams are functioning well, which is what makes their members satisfied and helps them progress quickly.

Summary

There are several important factors that can make you feel satisfied at work. These include

- Feeling appreciated for your work

- Having good relationships with your coworkers

- Maintaining a healthy work-life balance

- Having good relationships with your managers

- Working in a financially stable company

- Having opportunities for learning and career development

- Feeling secure in your job

- Earning a good salary

- Doing interesting work

- Sharing your company's values

- Feeling safe to take risks and make mistakes

- Being able to depend on your coworkers

- Having clear roles and goals

- Doing work that feels meaningful

- Seeing the impact of your work

- Ability to overcome being stuck with code

- Realistic deadlines

- Avoiding an "us vs. them" mentality

- Feeling invested in the company's success ("skin in the game")

Keep these factors in mind when you're deciding where you want to work and when you're trying to make your own team better.

References

[1]   www.news-sap.com/workforce-2020-looming-talent-crisis-research-shows-companies-unprepared-future-work/

[2]   https://blog.shrm.org/workforce/pay-jumps-to-top-factor-contributing-to-us-employees-satisfaction-with-thei

[3]   www.bcgperspectives.com/content/articles/human_resources_leadership_decoding_global_talent/

[4]   https://link.springer.com/chapter/10.1007/978-1-4842-4221-6_10

[5]   https://rework.withgoogle.com/print/guides/5721312655835136/

CHAPTER 2

Work Time Organization

Productivity as a software engineer can be influenced by many factors: the duration of your work hours, your level of focus, and the frequency and quality of your break. A well-structured workday helps to maximize your efficiency and reduces stress and burnout. It includes planning your tasks, setting realistic goals, taking regular breaks to rest, and minimizing distractions. It also involves maintaining a healthy work-life balance and ensuring that your professional responsibilities don't encroach on your personal time.

By structuring your workday effectively, you can achieve more in less time and with less effort. You can also improve your mental well-being, so, let's delve deeper into understanding the components of a well-structured workday and how you can implement them to enhance your productivity.

Working Hours

Imagine your typical eight-hour workday. Now, picture spending every minute of that time buried in code. Sounds overwhelming, doesn't it? That's because it is. We do a lot more than just coding during our work hours. We attend meetings, respond to emails, enjoy our lunch, and take breaks. The reality is that maintaining high productivity levels throughout an eight-hour coding marathon is almost impossible. I've only met a few

© Mykyta Chernenko 2023
M. Chernenko, *The Rational Software Engineer*,
https://doi.org/10.1007/978-1-4842-9795-7_2

people who can manage this pace, and those few tend to be extremely... well, let's say, geeky. For the rest of us mere mortals, coding nonstop for eight hours, particularly without any breaks, is a recipe for exhaustion.

Recognizing this, there's a growing movement [1] in some countries to reduce working hours from the standard 40. One recent success story comes from Iceland [2], where reducing the workweek to 35–36 hours has shown promising results. So, it seems less could indeed be more when it comes to working hours.

This brings us to a question: how much time does a software engineer actually spend writing code? When I asked my colleagues and friends, the consensus was that on their most productive, distraction-free days, they could code for about four to six hours max.

Now, if you whisper these figures to some managers (particularly the less experienced ones), you might just trigger a full-blown panic attack. "What on earth are they doing the rest of the time?!" they may ask. But here's the kicker: most of the people on their teams are likely coding even less than that. On average, employees spend only about 40% [3] on their primary work duties. And that doesn't even guarantee that this time is spent efficiently.

My personal target is five hours of **focused work** each day. If I have a stand-up meeting and a short lunch break at home, my working day can be as short as 5.5 hours. I feel great after such days since my output is good and I have plenty of leisure time afterward. But remember—it only works with five hours of focused work. Otherwise, you can work for more than ten hours and produce less output anyway.

However, my days don't usually total 5.5 hours. I try to be engaged with activities beyond just writing code and attending the daily stand-up meeting. If my day involves important calls, professional reading, knowledge-sharing sessions, and even a workout during the lunch break, my workday typically clocks in around the standard eight hours.

Some people might say that "you can never be the best if you only work for five hours," but I want to highlight that striving to be "the best" at one thing might not be the best goal. Trying to be the "best" at something often means sacrificing other areas of your life, especially considering the diminishing returns you get when you put in more effort beyond a certain point. Instead, being an outstanding tech expert is just one aspect of my life. I want to balance it with maintaining mental health, living a full life, and cultivating deep social connections. So, my goal is to be a pretty good, but more importantly, happy and fulfilled developer.

Focused Work

By "focused work" I mean the following thing: *I do the essential stuff and I work with a lot of concentration.*

Most of us struggle with discipline and are often distracted, which leads to spending time on nonessential tasks. Studies [4] indicate that checking news websites, scrolling social media, and chatting with colleagues can consume up to two hours of a typical workday. Furthermore, one in three people reports [5] spending two to five hours a day in unproductive meetings. I am not naturally great at staying focused, so I need to utilize effective techniques that help to reduce context switching and eliminate distractions, which I'm going to share next.

Meetings

Unless your presence is essential, skip meetings. If you're uncertain about your necessity at a meeting, chances are you don't need to be there. Although you may miss something semi-important occasionally, the time you save will more than compensate for it. One way to identify an ineffective meeting is the absence of a clear agenda, and you don't understand exactly what you are going to discuss. Be mindful of your time and the time of others. If you're the organizer, plan the meeting well, set a concise agenda, invite only necessary attendees, and provide a summary afterward.

Warning: There are some meetings you don't want to miss. For example, if the CEO of your company wants to share something, you might consider attending—even if there is no agenda and nobody knows what's gonna happen. (˘ ³˘)

Notifications

Notifications are evil [6] in terms of focus and productivity. Turn off your phone notifications and put your phone away to get rid of the temptation of checking it. Let's be honest, most of the notifications you get are not important and don't require your immediate reply. Your friends can wait for an answer whether you can join them at the bar, and a new breaking news title is just another clickbait.

Uninterrupted Time

It's important to create time to focus when you are not interrupted by colleagues either. A quick chat about a new version of Rust nightly and a question by a colleague that can be answered by googling for 15 seconds is not worth interruption and can wait until your break time. Book some time for your focused work in the calendar, turn on a "busy" status on Slack (or Do-not-Disturb alternative in your messenger), notify your team that you will be open for questions in an hour, or put a note on your head that you are busy.

Convey the information to others that you are not to be interrupted now. Some of the extreme programming proponents might disagree with this, but I believe that ad hoc meetings or hanging on a Discord channel all day long for immediate communication are often likely to bring more harm than benefits as they interrupt you. However, mind that if you don't respond to people, you can block other people's work. There are situations when a person cannot progress without your input, and it is fine if you are interrupted in such cases. Also, if your role is the lead of the team, team productivity is likely to be more important than your productivity. Being always available can be a valid option in such a case.

Also, grouping similar tasks together can help avoid context switching. For instance, if you have multiple emails to write, it might be more efficient to handle them all at once rather than drafting one every hour and having to repeatedly divert your focus away from other tasks.

Peak Productivity

You're most productive when you're fresh. Make use of this time for demanding cognitive tasks. Studies show [7] that our productivity wanes as the day progresses, so it's wise to utilize the first few work hours effectively for the most challenging tasks. I usually save this time for things that need a lot of focus and big-picture thinking as they use a lot of brain power and I want to do them as well as I can, for example, planning how to build a component or talking about architecture choices, or figuring out tricky bugs.

Prioritization

Prioritize ruthlessly. Establish your tasks for the day and adhere to the list. It may only take a few minutes to create, but it aids in tracking what needs to be done and what to prioritize. If your current activity doesn't contribute to the completion of your daily tasks, it may be unnecessary.

At the same time, relying on a first-in, first-out (FIFO) approach with the tasks that pop up during the day might lead you to focus primarily on immediate but unimportant tasks as these are commonly popular. One useful technique to improve the process is called Eisenhower Box which introduces the noting of importance and urgency to a task. The idea is to concentrate on tasks that are both urgent and important and then on important but not urgent tasks, but deprioritize unimportant tasks, and be mindful of spending most of the time on immediate unimportant tasks. Figure 2-1 shows the diagram of what we should do with a task by its category.

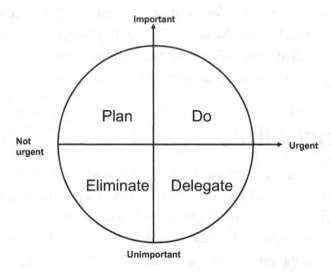

Figure 2-1. *Eisenhower Box illustrated*

A practical way to prioritize your tasks is to assign "urgency" and "importance" scores to each task on your to-do list and then multiply these values to determine priority. This method may be a simplification, but it generally works well for most tasks I encounter as a software engineer.

Write Things Down

Documenting things that arise during your day frees up your mental operating memory and aids in acting on discussions and commitments, as well as in prioritization. I try to jot down as much as makes sense, given my tendency to forget. The typical things I write down or create to-do lists for include

- Tasks I've promised to others.

- Things I need to follow up on but only want to revisit after finishing my current task, like a production warning or assisting someone with our project.

- Aspects I want to further explore in my code but tend to overlook, such as addressing a corner case, verifying compatibility with another system, or needing to provide additional testing for some part.

- Project-specific knowledge, like how to connect to our database through Bastion or architecture weaknesses in our code discovered during an incident investigation. I recall referring to my Notion notes at least five times a year to check how I can tunnel a database connection through a Kubernetes pod for local access.

I believe any note-taking app will suffice for a simple to-do list or small topic/details structure. However, if more organization is needed, it can be useful to employ more suitable tools. For instance, structuring a knowledge database using a database in Notion is one approach. Taking it a step further, the Zettelkasten method, which I describe in the Learning section of the book, can be highly effective.

Track and Measure

Sometimes we have a feeling that we have worked for a whole day, but when we are asked what exactly was accomplished, we don't have a clear answer. This can be an indicator that you were doing something nonessential. During the working day, you can write down what you were actually doing, for how long, and why you switched to the other activity. Look at the "activity" report at the end of the day. Ask yourself whether you have been working on the stuff you should have; if there were immediate tasks, what they were and why they appeared; and if you didn't accomplish your task list, what hampered you to achieve it. You will likely find something you can eliminate to improve your productivity.

If you find it difficult to keep track of your actions, you can install a tracking system on your machine, which would take screenshots every 5/10/20 minutes, so that you'll be able to look at the "report" after work and see your distractions. There is a startup called Rewind that basically records all the info you have on the screen; you can scroll it back to find what you have been doing. There are also apps such as RescueTime and Rize that are trying to record and classify what you are doing by a category or app. However, be careful as such tools can go against the security rules of your company or even break a privacy law if you record a meeting without explicit consent.

Overtime, Brrr, No Thanks

Overworking not only severely reduces our output, but it also comes with health risks and job dissatisfaction [8], not to mention increased levels of stress and fatigue [9]. Furthermore, every additional hour put to work brings less and less returns when you are already tired. Personally, I find that after six focused hours of work in a day, my mental clarity starts to wane. The more I try to force myself to keep working, the less motivated I become.

However, we all understand that crunch times can occasionally occur—working longer hours to meet a release deadline, fixing a critical production bug affecting users, or attending a late, urgent meeting all of these can actually be fun on their own if they happen occasionally. The key here is **occasionally**. If you consistently find yourself in a crunch before every release, troubleshooting bugs late into the night after most production releases, or having late meetings multiple times per week, it shows a serious issue with your processes or your management. The solution? Improve those processes or talk to your manager!

For instance, I once worked on a project involving numerous interconnected microservices in an "event-driven architecture." Whenever we deployed one microservice, we had to test the entire pipeline end to end—the only way to ensure everything functioned together. This was particularly problematic as several teams were working concurrently and the shifting contract between microservices was often a point of failure.

If the pipeline broke post-release, our first response was to revert the last commit and redeploy, minimizing downtime while investigating the issue. This cycle—waiting for the CI/CD process to complete, testing the pipeline, making another revert commit, waiting again, and retesting—often took over an hour, leading to unwanted overtime.

My solution? I spent two days writing the first end-to-end test that would run before deployment. After that, I no longer had to wait and manually check the pipeline post-release. I knew that if there was an error, it simply wouldn't be deployed. This process improvement eliminated unnecessary overtime and made the end of my workday more predictable, and I've seen similar strategies effectively mitigate overtime in many other situations.

And it goes without saying that explaining to your manager that constant overtime doesn't fit with your desired work-life balance is a thing that should be met with respect. If your employer expects you to overwork and it is far from what you want to do constantly, it is a good reason to leave.

What about working from home? It can be even harder to control that you don't work overtime. I've seen plenty of developers say something along the lines of "It feels like I don't work from home—I live at work. There is no clear separation between home and work anymore." One good recommendation that prevents me from getting into a loop of constant overtime work is to make plans right after your working hours. For example, since I finish at 4:00 p.m., I tend to make some plans for 5:00 p.m.: booking a gym time, getting together with a friend, or booking a table at a restaurant. That ensures that I finish on time most days. Obviously, if I have to work overtime to fix the production that I screwed up myself, I can cancel my arrangement, but if it's just a "very important" meeting on whether we should introduce a new JavaScript library to handle price formatting or write the functionality ourselves at 4:30 pm, then, sorry, but I am on my way to the gym.

And there is one small but important point: If I work for 12 hours per day, I simply cannot do other enjoyable activities. And I bet you want to live life besides the job too.

Rest for Your Own Sake

Aiming for five hours of focused work per day doesn't mean you should accomplish it in one sitting. In fact, frequent breaks are beneficial as they help you maintain productivity over the long term [11]. The well-known Pomodoro Technique [12] can be handy. Having work cycles of approximately 50 minutes followed by about 15 minutes of rest is a good beginning [13].

If you find it challenging to concentrate for a solid 50 minutes, you might consider using a free app like "Forest: Stay Focused" or a similar alternative. "Forest" suppresses phone notifications and incorporates an element of gamification into the process. I used it for a while but stopped after realizing that I had no significant issue concentrating for 30–50 minutes on my own.

Also, I don't generally monitor the duration of one "cycle" of work and rest, and I simply take a brief break whenever I feel the need. This approach works for me, but you might find it easier to manage your time in a more structured manner.

When choosing an activity for your rest periods, try to select something that is fundamentally different from your main work tasks. Engaging in cognitive tasks such as writing code during work and reading documentation during rest periods can be exhausting. Both activities require considerable mental effort and don't provide a true "break" for your brain.

However, engaging in physical activities or creative pursuits during your breaks can help to get back. Activities such as exercise, meditation, taking a walk, singing, playing a musical instrument, or even just having a casual conversation can serve as effective rest activities.

Combine Different Activities

It's not always about writing code. There are a lot more activities that you can do at work, and I find it more productive and entertaining to combine them. Writing code for five hours per day can yield good output, but if I work like that for five days per week, I can get a bit bored. I enjoy the days when I can write code for three to four hours and spend three to four hours writing articles, mentoring, interviewing, learning and mentoring, knowledge sharing, and many other activities. Being involved in different activities also makes me more satisfied with my work in general.

Education

I highly recommend setting aside dedicated time for education during your workweek. A commitment of three to five hours per week is a good starting point, and it's beneficial to physically book this time in your calendar to avoid interruptions during your learning sessions.

If your company does not currently have a common practice of dedicating time to employee education, consider discussing and promoting this idea with your manager. From my experience, it's not as difficult as it might sound. Most organizations recognize the value of continuous learning and development, and they often appreciate employees who show initiative in this regard.

Work from Home

The COVID-19 pandemic ushered in a significant shift in work dynamics, with many people transitioning to working from home. Some found this change positive, for example, this study shows that people in the WFH group quit 50% less often and took fewer sick days [14]. Others have experienced challenges in organizing their space, being productive, and feeling community.

When you're working from home, here are a few tips to consider:

- **Designate a Workspace**: Try to associate a specific space in your house with work. Dedicate a corner solely for work-related activities; this can make it easier to concentrate on work when you're in that space and disconnect when you leave it at the end of your working schedule. If possible, consider setting up a dedicated room to serve as your "home office."

- **Invest in Quality Work Equipment**: Make your workplace comfortable. While not everyone might find this essential, many people believe that a good table, a comfortable chair, and a couple of monitors are must-haves. Many companies provide a special budget for setting up your home office—take advantage of it if you can. Your spine and eyes are your breadmakers, just like fingers are for a pianist. Don't go cheap on them.

- **Maintain Social Connections**: Remote work can be socially challenging, and it's easy to forget that you're part of a team. Try to meet your colleagues from time to time. If possible and if you're comfortable with it, aim to meet your colleagues in person once every two weeks and spend some quality time together.

Personally, I appreciate both traditional office work and remote work, and I believe a combination of both would be ideal. Working from home allows me to exercise, shower, cook, rest, and avoid distractions more comfortably. I also save at least an hour that would otherwise be spent commuting. On the other hand, I find that I feel slightly more motivated when I'm in a physical office. I enjoy interacting with my team in person, and certain activities like workshops, interviews, mentoring sessions, and knowledge-sharing sessions tend to be more efficient when conducted face-to-face. Therefore, if your circumstances allow, aim to leverage the best of both worlds.

How to Handle Procrastination

Procrastination is a significant obstacle to productivity and good mental health [16]. It also feels extremely unpleasant—you feel guilty and that you are a fool, which is a self-sabotaging self, so self-loathing creeps in fairly quickly.

Many of the strategies outlined before can help you manage "simple" procrastination cases, such as getting distracted or struggling with general time management. However, there may still be tasks that trigger intense procrastination. In these situations, I employ a variety of techniques to overcome these potent procrastination triggers:

1. **Recognize Procrastination**: The first step is to acknowledge when you're procrastinating. This can be tricky because procrastination can be masked by focusing on "other" tasks. If you feel the urge to

complete a nonessential or less important task when you know you should be focusing on something else, that's hidden procrastination.

2. **Break Tasks Down**: It's challenging to start a cognitively demanding task that requires 30 hours of coding time. But starting with preliminary research, clarifying aspects of the task, or writing one test case usually feels more manageable. If it's tough to break down a large task into logical chunks, you can still divide it into time buckets. Agreeing to work with a focus for 20 minutes on a daunting task is often a lot more achievable. This approach can trick your brain and get you into a state where you finish a small task, and once you're already in motion, it's easier to continue.

3. **Establish Accountability**: This approach may not be the most comfortable one, but it can be necessary at times. Essentially, it involves creating a clear promise to yourself or somebody else about how much and when you will do something. Be cautious with this technique, though, as it's a potent quick-fix method that can potentially lead to burnout.

4. **Understand the Causes of Procrastination**: In the long run, it's vital to practice mindfulness about your procrastination. This means trying to understand the deeper reasons why you're procrastinating. When I experience prolonged bouts of procrastination, I focus on identifying the underlying thoughts and feelings that are causing it. Are you afraid of failure? Do you feel overwhelmed

by the task's size? Do you need help or support to complete the task? Do you find the task boring, unmotivating, or frustrating? Identifying the root cause makes it much easier to address the problem. If procrastination becomes a systemic psychological issue, therapeutic approaches like cognitive behavioral therapy (CBT) or acceptance and commitment therapy (ACT) are effective in dealing with procrastination.

There's a more scholarly way to define procrastination. Tim Pychyl, in his series, "Solving the Procrastination Puzzle," on the Waking Up app, says, "Procrastination is a voluntary delay of an intended action despite expecting to be worse off because of the delay." In other words, we know doing something is the best choice, but we still avoid it.

At its core, procrastination is a problem with handling emotions. We often think doing the task will be worse than it actually is and not doing it will feel better than it really does. A helpful book on this topic is "Affect Regulation Training" [17]. It talks about how to regulate our emotions and provides a growing body of research that proves its effectiveness [18].

Here are the steps:

1. Relax your muscles.

2. Slow down your breath.

3. Watch your thoughts and emotions without judging them.

4. Accept your emotions as they are.

5. Be kind to yourself, and avoid feeling guilty.

6. Understand what's causing these emotions.

7. Change the emotions that distress you.

I've explained each point in more detail in the podcast series I mentioned at the start. But remember, these steps require a lot of practice. In fact, studies show it takes six weeks to effectively learn all seven steps. Usually, therapists' work is needed on the last two steps.

All of that being said, keep in mind that sometimes procrastination is just a good sign that you don't enjoy what you're doing. In that case, you might need to consider what you should do to stop doing it altogether.

Habits

While many of the strategies I've mentioned might be new to you, and integrating them into your work routine may seem like a daunting task, forming new habits can make the process much easier. James Clear's excellent book, "Atomic Habits," provides many insightful tips on breaking negative habits and building new, beneficial ones. Here are a few that I find particularly useful:

- **Form New Identity**: Identify yourself as someone who values work-life balance, happiness, and productivity. Some people say this is the most powerful tool. When you present a certain image to yourself and others, you strive to live up to it. Just like it's harder to quit running if you say you are a runner, it's the same with maintaining satisfaction at work when you see and present yourself as someone who cares about it.

- **Use Habit Cues**: Habit cues can make it easier to engage in desired behaviors. For example, if you want to do a short exercise before lunch, place your exercise equipment near your dining table. This will serve as a reminder to do your workout. If you're trying to implement the Pomodoro Technique, stick an image of a tomato (pomodoro in Italian) on an alarm clock and place it on your desk.

- **Habit Stacking**: Habit stacking involves chaining habits together, so the completion of one habit triggers the start of another. This strategy can help you establish a routine where each action naturally leads to the next.

- **Start Small**: Begin with very small actions. If you find the idea of a 50-minute, distraction-free focus session daunting, start with just ten minutes (or less) and gradually increase the duration as you get used to it.

Artificial Intelligence (AI)

AI and LLMs have significantly enhanced productivity. There are many tools available today that can help improve performance. Some tools automatically schedule events on your calendar, while LLMs can even write code for you. Among these, LLMs are currently the standout performers.

A study by BCG [19] highlighted that consultants who utilized GPT-4 managed to

- Complete 12% more tasks

- Work 25% faster

- Improve the quality of their output by 40%

Although the tasks performed by business consultants differ from those of developers, LLMs are invaluable tools for us. However, it's essential to be cautious and not over-rely on LLMs. Their output should be seen as a step in the process, not the end result.

To give you an idea of how GPT-4 can assist in coding, here are areas where it excels and where it might not be as helpful:

Good at

- **Writing Scripts:** For example, "Open a file called x.csv, and import the data in our PostgreSQL database, write it in Python."

- **Converting from One Format to Another:** For example, "Here is a JSON structure of my Grafana dashboard "...", and here are the definitions of the Terraform resources "...". Convert my JSON structure to Terraform."

- **Writing Functions Under 300 Lines with Few Dependencies:** For example, "Write a function in Go that accepts a string in the format "some words {{variable_a}}, {{ b }}. Another sentence" and extracts all variable names inside "{{" and "}}" into an array of variables, then returns it."

- **DSLs, Query Languages:** For example, "Here is a structure of my PostgreSQL tables "....". Write a query that gets the average feedback score by day from the 9th of September to now."

- **Debugging Issues:** For example, "I try to parse this yaml file "...". Here are my Zod structure definitions "...". Here is the error: "...". What is wrong?"

- **Explaining Tech Concepts:** For example, "I don't understand space-based architecture. Please, explain it to me with an example of a web ecommerce system."

Bad at

- **Recent Knowledge, New Libraries, Changing Formats:** For example, "Rewrite the code to use the most recent dependencies for my React Native project."

- **Debugging Environment-Specific Issues:** For example, "When I try to install this package with pnpm, I get this error "...". What is wrong?"

Summary

- On productive, distraction-free days, software engineers can code for about four to six hours.

- Set aside time for focused work without interruptions.

- Notify users that you are having a focus bout, so you don't get distracted.

- Have good meeting hygiene, avoid unnecessary meetings, and ensure any meetings attended have a clear agenda.

- Turn off your notifications when you are trying to focus.

- Make use of fresh hours for demanding cognitive tasks.

- Assign "urgency" and "importance" scores to each task to determine priority.

- Write down tasks, follow-ups, and other points of interest to free up mental memory and aid in prioritization.

- Write down what tasks you're working on, their duration, and reasons for switching activities. Review these at the end of the day.

- Be aware of your work hours, and aim to avoid consistent overwork. If you're frequently working overtime, identify and address the issues causing it.

- To avoid overworking when working from home, plan activities after work hours to ensure a clear end to your workday.

- Implement a system of regular breaks during your workday. Consider using techniques like the Pomodoro Technique.

- Break up your workday by engaging in a variety of tasks like coding, writing, mentoring, interviewing, and knowledge sharing.

- Set aside a few hours per week for education and continuous learning.

- If you're working from home, create a specific space for work-related activities.

- Recognize when you're procrastinating, break tasks down into manageable parts, establish accountability, and understand the root cause of your procrastination.

- Implement strategies from "Atomic Habits" like habit cues, habit stacking, and starting small to form new, positive habits.

- Explore how LLMs can help you to generate better code, do it quicker, and help you learn.

References

[1] www.independent.co.uk/news/business/six-hour-work-day-increases-productivity-so-will-britain-and-america-adopt-one-sweden-a7066961.html

[2] https://en.alda.is/wp-content/uploads/2021/07/ICELAND_4DW.pdf

[3] Report_2018-2019-State-of-Work-report-FINAL.pdf (workfront.com)

[4] www.inc.com/melanie-curtin/in-an-8-hour-day-the-average-worker-is-productive-for-this-many-hours.html

[5] www.kornferry.com/about-us//press/working-or-wasting-time

[6] www.sciencedaily.com/releases/2015/07/150709133044.htm

[7] www.researchgate.net/publication/315670177_Working_Hours_and_Productivity

[8] www.employment-studies.co.uk/report-summaries/report-summary-working-long-hours-review-evidence-volume-1-%E2%80%93-main-report

[9] www.hse.gov.uk/research/hsl_pdf/2003/hsl03-02.pdf

[10] http://ftp.iza.org/dp8129.pdf

[11] https://news.cornell.edu/stories/1999/09/onscreen-break-reminder-boosts-productivity

[12] https://en.wikipedia.org/wiki/Pomodoro_Technique

[13] www.theatlantic.com/business/archive/2014/09/science-tells-you-how-many-minutes-should-you-take-a-break-for-work-17/380369/

[14] www.nber.org/system/files/working_papers/w18871/w18871.pdf

[15] https://app.wakingup.com/content/PKOAA14

[16] Longitudinal Study of Procrastination, Performance, Stress, and
      Health: The Costs and Benefits of Dawdling - Dianne M Tice, Roy
      F. Baumeister, 1997 (sagepub.com)

[17] https://link.springer.com/book/10.1007/978-1-4939-1022-9

[18] www.ncbi.nlm.nih.gov/pmc/articles/PMC6715183/

[19] https://papers.ssrn.com/sol3/papers.cfm?abstract_id=4573321

CHAPTER 3

There Is No Perfect Project

Imagine a software engineer you've probably come across. Let's call him Bob. Every day, you hear him grumbling about his team's lack of skill, and dull tasks, and saying things like "This isn't my job!" or "The managers don't know what they're doing!" Sound familiar? Bob seems angry and unhappy with his project, clearly not satisfied. If you ask him if he likes the project, he'll say, "Absolutely not!" Even if you ask him to name ONE thing he likes about the project, he'll have a hard time coming up with something. You might think Bob should change jobs because he's obviously in a bad place. So, he does. He leaves his old job with a string of complaints and starts a new "dream" project. But guess what? After a few weeks, he's back to complaining. The same old story. This happens because **the problem isn't the project—it's Bob**.

Now, let's meet Alice. Every so often, she'll share a story about a colleague's mistake or a manager who acted poorly. But she doesn't complain or get angry. Instead, it's just a lighthearted story to share over lunch. Overall, Alice is happy with her project even though she'd change a few things if she could. She says she's learning a lot and that she can reach her personal goals on the project if she works hard. Alice thinks about switching projects when she feels she's not growing as fast and can't learn much more—like when she keeps doing the same tasks repeatedly. When she moves to a new "dream" project, she finds it has its own set of

© Mykyta Chernenko 2023
M. Chernenko, *The Rational Software Engineer*,
https://doi.org/10.1007/978-1-4842-9795-7_3

challenges. But that's okay. Alice understands this is normal and knows she can still gain a lot from the project. *She acknowledges the weaknesses of the project but doesn't let them spoil the fun.*

What's funny is that these two characters can be on the same project, doing pretty much the same tasks. But while Alice will stay positive and satisfied with her career, Bob will always be chasing the impossible "perfect" project.

This simple understanding has made my life much easier. Yes, I'll meet people I don't enjoy interacting with, project requirements will change when I least expect it, and I might have to pick up tasks that someone else "should be doing." If I keep chasing a "perfect" project, I might never find it and end up feeling disappointed throughout my career. So, the advice I give myself is, "Stop searching for the 'perfect' project. Instead, make an 'average' one enjoyable."

You'll work on various projects throughout your career, and you won't like all of them equally. They'll vary in quality and have different flaws, but if you approach them sensibly, you can learn a lot—even from a "bad" project.

Don't get me wrong, I'm not saying you should put up with a poor work environment. If you're stressed out after each workday and your project has driven you to rely on a mix of sedatives and antidepressants just to feel okay, then you likely need to change something. I'll explain later what I consider to be red flags. But for now, understand that **a certain level of imperfection is acceptable**.

How to Effectively Onboard on a New Project

Since a "perfect" project is more of a dream than a reality, how do we handle an "ordinary" project with all its flaws? The answer lies in adapting our approach, and a well-thought-out strategy is essential for this.
I split my strategy creation into four parts: **inception, goals, actions, and monitoring**.

Inception is when I familiarize myself with the project and the work environment. I try to understand the people I'll be working with, what others like and dislike about the project, the project's technology stack, and what unique and valuable experience I can gain here. It might take me a month or even more to feel comfortable in the project and to get to know most of the people I'll be interacting with. During this period, I avoid making quick judgments or drawing negative conclusions. A lot of project weaknesses turn out to make much more sense after I get enough context and feel less frustrating with time as new opportunities to mitigate them pop up.

Goals are the general things I aim to achieve on the project and the negative outcomes I want to avoid. For instance, "I want to learn more about distributed architecture, and I don't want to be involved in gathering requirements." My goals should align with my overall career path and development plan. For example, if I aspire to be a Tech Lead, the goals I set for the project should help me progress toward this role. Some examples could be the following:

- Learn a new technology, architecture, or development approach used in the project.

- Gain knowledge and experience in management, mentoring, or software architecture.

- Work without overtime.

- Increase the satisfaction level of other employees.

Most often, my project goals fall into two main categories: gaining valuable knowledge and maintaining a good work experience on the project. The former usually helps with my personal goals, and the latter is achieved by mitigating the project's weaknesses.

Actions are the specific steps I take to achieve these goals. One goal may require several actions. For example, "work without overtime" might involve explaining my values to management or optimizing the testing approach so I don't have to stay late fixing critical bugs.

Monitoring is the ongoing process of adjusting my goals and actions on the project, lasting until I finish working on the project. Interests can change and new opportunities may arise as the project evolves. I can't plan everything from the start, so my goals and actions need to adapt to new information and opportunities. Often, half of the goals on my list only emerge after a few months of working on the project.

Personally, I keep track of all these strategy steps in my head without writing them down. However, making notes or using tools like to-do lists can be really helpful in keeping track of your goals and actions.

Next, I'll share two examples of how I've managed "imperfect" projects and what my strategy looked like, dividing the information into the four sections I just described.

Strategy in a Chaotic Startup Environment

The first project was a startup aiming to provide AI-based insights from news articles, tweets, and more, which I joined as a consultant. There were multiple teams, each focusing on different aspects of the system.

Inception:

With the project being somewhat chaotic and requirements changing frequently, getting up to speed and identifying my goals were a challenge. Some opportunities only surfaced when the system's core developers left, which allowed me to take over parts of the system I was interested in.

Weaknesses:

- High turnover, leading to situations where no one had enough knowledge about certain parts of the system to change or fix them.

- Chaotic requirements, to the point where my main daily task could be changed multiple times.

- Demanding but ineffective management that often pushed for overtime.

Strengths:

- Powerful CI/CD infrastructure that was new to me.

- Architectural patterns I had little experience with.

- With some initiative on my part, I could take over complex parts of the system and learn from them.

Goals for the project:

- Gain as much DevOps experience as possible as it was the project's most valuable aspect in terms of knowledge.

- Learn more about the architectural patterns in use, and understand their practical pros and cons.

- Avoid all overtime caused by poor management.

- Take over the most complex parts of the projects or those using technologies I hadn't tried yet.

- Leave the project once I've extracted most of the available knowledge.

Actions:

- Deploy my solutions myself, and assist data science in deploying theirs.

- Review existing CI/CD solutions, and ask DevOps to explain how they work and why they're designed that way.

- Implement new solutions using the event-driven architecture paradigm, and compare the results to similar solutions I would implement in a monolithic architecture.

- Decline meetings outside of my working hours.

- Regularly remind the client that my overtime will be charged extra.

- Provide estimates for management's "immediate" tasks with a bit of a buffer. As a result, they could see how it could affect the scope of the sprint and couldn't blame me—all their "tiny immediate" tasks were recorded in Jira.

- Be proactive about new technologies and approaches that could meet new requirements.

- Align with my consultancy company that I'm not enthusiastic about staying on the project for more than a couple of months.

- Leave the project when I understand most of it and have had a lot of hands-on experience with new technologies.

Results:

- I built several CI/CD solutions for my team and helped the data science team with their machine learning model CI/CD.

- I went through most of the CI/CD infrastructure and gained a good understanding of how they worked.

- During the six months I worked on this project, I only worked overtime for about two weeks in total, and even then, it was just a few hours extra, not over the weekend.

- I built a new API and pipeline using the event-driven paradigm.

- I built a Data Lake + ETL using AWS-hosted solutions, with no prior knowledge of either.

- I gained some experience with Kubeflow.

- I learned a significant amount about Terraform and Kubernetes.

- I moved from the project almost as soon as my progress began to slow.

This project had plenty of flaws: ineffective management, an overbearing work culture, a lack of processes for code reviews, retrospectives, project planning, requirement gathering, product discovery, and much more. It epitomized the type of "startup environment" many people try to avoid. Despite this, I gained valuable knowledge from it, maintained high levels of motivation, and didn't work excessive overtime.

Interestingly, this project also demonstrated how crucial attitude and strategy are for job satisfaction. I worked with five other consultants from my company on the project, all of whom seemed unhappy and complained frequently. Meanwhile, I was quite content with the project and, most importantly, gained a lot of valuable knowledge.

Strategy on a Project with a Big Time Zone Difference and Little Trust

The project aimed to provide software for seamless clusterization, involving a lot of custom close-to-hardware solutions, a large team of software engineers, and complex architecture.

Inception:

- I realized I had little control over my team and tasks.

- I was assigned full-time automation testing instead of development, contrary to my expectations, and I was not pleased.

- Soon, I had the opportunity to switch to a smaller subproject where the management was more competent, and meetings were useful and infrequent.

Weaknesses:

- With a ten-hour time difference from the main office, I initially had three to four weekly meetings at 7:00–8:00 p.m., which interfered with my personal plans.

- I quickly realized that nobody trusted me with complicated parts of the system because I was a consultant and had less experience than the core team. Some of the things I didn't manage to change till the very end. For example, for a reason I still don't understand, I was not given VPN access for the whole nine months I worked on the project (even though all of my other consultant colleagues got access). I had to use Remote Desktop Access to access Jira instead. If you have ever used Remote Desktop Access to a computer located halfway around the globe, you know how painful it is. It would take me ten minutes to change the status of a task in Jira. My manager would simply ignore my messages about VPN access.

- The processes were slow, sometimes painfully so. For example, receiving SSH keys could take weeks. It took four months of persistent communication with the management to respond to my strong desire to stop writing automation tests.

Strengths:

- The project was technically complex and used various new technologies, providing a wealth of learning opportunities.

- There were several excellent engineers on the team from whom I could learn.

Goals:

- Minimize pointless late meetings.

- Gain trust to be assigned more challenging tasks.

- Gain hands-on experience with TypeScript and Go.

- Cease working as an AQA.

- Learn from skilled engineers on the project.

Actions:

- Get rid of unnecessary meetings by switching subprojects.

- Demonstrate competence through initiative and good code.

- Aim to work more with TypeScript and Go subprojects rather than Python-based ones.

- Strive to work with people I could learn from.

- Express my dissatisfaction with working as an AQA to both my company's management and the project's management.

- Focus on self-education.

- Learn the project's code base and architecture, even parts I didn't need but was interested in.

- Be more involved in company activities that I enjoyed more than AQA, such as mentoring, writing articles, and knowledge sharing.

- Change my schedule and move some plans from evening to morning.

Results:

- One to two useful late meetings per week instead of three to four pointless ones.

- After four months, I stopped doing AQA and started working on the development of new, challenging features.

- I was eventually assigned to the team of talented engineers I wanted to learn from.

- Gained hands-on experience with both Go and TypeScript.

- A deeper understanding of distributed systems and the technologies used to build them.

- Managed to avoid burnout.

This project was mentally the most challenging experience for me. Working as an AQA for a few months, rewriting my implementations multiple times due to last-minute changes in requirements, feeling that my work had little impact, dealing with late meetings, and being ignored by the management did not contribute to my satisfaction. However, I was not unhappy either. I still learned a lot, managed to do plenty of self-education and enjoyable side activities, and in the end, worked with people I saw as role models.

Takeaways from the Example

As you can see, even though the projects I listed were not sweet dreams, it was still possible for me to grow with their helm, get useful experience, and keep my mind stable.

When I see something on a project and I cannot change it myself, there are two strategies that I turn to, either to change something or to leave. Let's talk about them in more detail.

Talk to the Management First

If I find a project challenging because I'm not growing as I'd like, I'm dealing with a difficult colleague, or I want something changed, I talk to my manager. Companies usually have many ways to keep their software engineers happy. They could let you switch to a different part of the project, change the technology you're working with, raise your pay, or even let go of someone who's hard to work with (especially if you're not the only one who feels this way). There's a good solution or a fair compromise for every problem, well, at least for most problems. :)

Diversify Your Time

Even if the project I'm working on isn't that fun, there're a lot of other things I can do at the company. These other tasks can help me grow and also help the company. Plus, they keep me interested for a longer time. For example, I might spend a month writing CSS, but if I also do different tasks within the company, I can stay interested for several months. If I notice I'm not learning enough about something from the project, I can learn on my own, use the company's library, or start a side project.

At Times the Best Option Is to Leave

Imagine a Buddhist monk who has studied and earned a PhD in machine learning, followed by five years of work on state-of-the-art projects involving challenging tasks and pleasant working environments. Now, place this monk on a project that primarily involves CSS fixes to meet the requirements of the pixel-perfect design, supervised by a toxic boss, a low salary, and a 12-hour workday. Can the monk maintain calm and happiness in such conditions? Monks might (though, honestly, even a Buddhist monk might crack under this pressure). But the question is, "**Why should they**?" when they can simply quit and find a better project?

I certainly don't possess the equanimity or tolerance of most Buddhist monks, and I guess neither do you. So the question becomes, "Is the project worth dealing with all of its troubles?" Sometimes the answer is, "No, I give more than I get in return." Then it's reasonable to leave. This may seem obvious, but I've met many people who still won't leave a project even when they believe they should.

There are two main categories of reasons why I might leave a company: either I cannot meet my goals as a software engineer on the project, or I find the project's working environment unbearable. If I've tried to change things and failed, it's time to exit.

If I can't develop in the direction I desire on a project and I can't change that, it's a clear sign I should find something else. For instance, if I aim to grow as a back-end developer but am assigned to the front-end role on the project and know I won't be able to change that for the next year, I'm not progressing toward my personal goals.

An unbearable working environment can include various factors: an expectation of overtime, toxic management, company values that don't align with mine, a significant time zone difference, or a low salary. If I can't mitigate or embrace one of these factors and the project's benefits aren't worth it, I would also consider leaving the company.

At the start of the article, I mentioned Bob who has a negative attitude toward a project without a valid reason. However, there's another group of software engineers at the opposite end of the spectrum—those who are unhappy with their project for a valid reason, yet they continue to work on it. Your goals as a software engineer and your overall well-being are the main concerns you should prioritize. So know when you should leave, and don't tolerate what you shouldn't.

Summary

- Accept that a "perfect" project is a myth. Every project has its flaws, and the key lies in managing these imperfections effectively.

- Transform an "imperfect" project into a "good" one.

- Create and implement an adaptation strategy, which should include inception, goal-setting, action-taking, and constant monitoring.

- Ensure that the goals of your project align with your broader career objectives as a software engineer.

- Engage in side activities to diversify your workload and fill any gaps that your primary project might not cover.

- Communicate openly with your manager any concerns or issues you might have.

- Know when it's time to move on. Leaving a project when necessary is an important aspect of your career progression.

CHAPTER 4

Initiative

Taking the initiative at work is something I genuinely enjoy. By "initiative," I mean bringing new concepts, ideas, methods, or processes to the table or stepping up to tackle some new, exciting, or challenging task that could be put off. It seems that it is not only my observation; this research [1] shows that taking initiative correlates well with job satisfaction. It might not be a direct cause and effect, but it's a winning combo for me.

For instance, while being on the project with little trust, I decided to entertain myself with various activities within the company. I wrote articles, mentored folks, helped put together a conference, and even gave mentees a hand with English lessons. The drive to do all these things sprang from my own initiative. I asked my company where I could be useful so that I could shift my focus away from the main project.

But being proactive isn't just about having fun—it usually benefits the team and the company, too. If you identify a systematic problem in your company, which affects you negatively and you can solve it with an initiative—that's an amazing opportunity. You help both yourself and your company. It is a typical win-win attitude that I'm trying to stick to.

Fixing What Is Broken

Participating in activities isn't just about fun, it can also be a powerful tool for solving real issues that are impacting your work enjoyment. Imagine this: your company's important info is scattered across 30 different Slack channels, and you're spending 10–30 minutes to find a guide, like how

© Mykyta Chernenko 2023
M. Chernenko, *The Rational Software Engineer*,
https://doi.org/10.1007/978-1-4842-9795-7_4

to rotate SSL certificate secret keys. Not exactly enjoying, right? And this situation flags a systemic issue in the company. If you propose and implement a solution, like a centralized knowledge database, you will not only make your life easier, you will also help out the whole company.

Being proactive like this can also help avoid feeling like a victim, which rarely leads anywhere good. For instance, at one of my companies, we didn't proper HR department, so there was no one to organize team-building activities. This was during the COVID-19 pandemic, so the problem felt even worse. We barely saw each other, and there was no budget for social events. We could have spent ages complaining about this in the team, but that wouldn't have fixed anything. Instead, we emphasized to our manager the importance of setting aside a budget for fun activities and took the lead by organizing a simple get-together at a local café and a walk after that. This sparked a trend in other teams, and management eventually agreed to introduce dedicated team budgets for social activities.

Side Activities

There are plenty of activities that one can get involved in a company. Let's get through some of them to give you inspiration:

- **Reading Technical Blogs/Articles**: This is a great way to stay updated with the latest trends and technologies in the industry.

- **Online Courses**: There are numerous online platforms offering courses on various technical topics. Choose one that aligns with your career goals.

- **Coding Challenges**: Websites like HackerRank, LeetCode, or Codewars host coding challenges that help improve problem-solving skills.

- **Open Source Contribution**: Contributing to open source projects not only helps improve your coding skills but also brings back tribute to the community.

- **Writing Technical Blogs**: This helps consolidate your understanding of topics and also improves your communication skills.

- **Mentoring**: If you have somebody who needs your knowledge in your company, mentoring them can be a fulfilling task that also helps you reinforce your own knowledge.

- **Building a Personal Project**: This helps you apply what you've learned and play around with new technologies

- **Networking**: Engage with colleagues, attend meetups, or participate in online communities.

- **Listening to Podcasts**: There are many tech podcasts that can provide you with industry insights during your downtime.

- **Reading Books**: There are numerous excellent technical and nontechnical books that can expand your knowledge and perspectives.

- **Documenting Your Work**: Good documentation skills are highly valued in any software engineering role.

- **Organizing or Participating in Hackathons**: This is both fun and a great learning experience.

- **Giving Tech Talks**: Sharing your knowledge with others helps you understand concepts better. Plus, if you're reading books or articles during your work hours, bringing the knowledge back to the company creates a win-win situation for everybody.

- **Getting Involved in the Interview Process**: Interviewing people is an art in itself, and it is a skill that is useful for almost every company.

- **Participating or Organizing the R&D Team**: If you have a cutting-edge idea and need some technical resources to help you build it, try to join the R&D team in your company or initiate one.

- **Joining an Internal Committee**: Employee committees, such as fun, technical groups, or innovation, can help enhance your leadership and organizational skills while contributing to what matters to the company.

- **Internal Tool Development**: Creating tools that improve internal processes can save time for the whole team and improve motivation if it automatizes a repetitive manual task.

- **Customer Interactions**: Directly interacting with customers can provide valuable insights into what they think and expect from your product.

- **Training on Company Products/Services**: Deep understanding of what your company provides to the end users gives insights that help to understand the choices the company makes better and how you can efficiently contribute to its success.

- **Whatever Else Is Beneficial and Interesting for You to Do in the Company**: Each company is different, and I'm sure if you look around well enough, you will find a dozen of interesting side activities you participate in.

How Initiatives Can Bring Unexpected Results

Taking initiative may appear as merely a diversion from your primary tasks, seemingly not adding immediate value. However, I strongly contest this view. Every act of initiative, every non-programming activity you engage in, has the potential to open up doors to something great. One mentoring session might not yield significant outcomes immediately, but if you undertake a hundred different activities over three years, the odds of something exceptional happening increase dramatically.

For example, you dedicate some time to learning C in your spare time, and down the line, that knowledge assists you in landing on the new exciting IoT R&D project within your company because they need somebody who can get deeper into the hardware optimizations. Or, your involvement in some product management tasks ends up paving the way for a management position or even lays the foundation for your own startup.

Here's an example from my own experience. I once decided to extend my mentoring program beyond programming and helped a mentee improve his English, complete with actionable steps and a timeline. This experience raised my interest in teaching, prompting me to go deeper into the subject. Fast-forward a bit, and I found myself using this newfound knowledge to help a friend through coaching sessions to land a new job and join a volunteering organization to teach kids to write in Scratch. Eventually, the coaching and teaching skills I acquired became useful in my role as a Tech Lead. Had I not taken the initiative to guide my mentee in English learning, I wouldn't have gained this valuable skill and interest that's been so beneficial in my career.

Another story. When I first joined a product team, I got curious about product management. It didn't seem directly useful for my career right then, but I enjoyed learning about it. I started to help with some product-related tasks, and that gave me some good experience. I've also read a few books on the topic, started following a few impressive figures in the field with amazing insights, and started discussing the topic more with people. All of that seemed mostly like an interest that I couldn't apply to my immediate position. But after two months, when I started exploring ideas for my startup, product management experience came in handy as it provided a good foundation of knowledge that I could build on top. If I hadn't had it, I'm sure that I would have selected a much worse idea to work on as I would not have had enough knowledge how to validate product ideas correctly.

The most thrilling moments in my career and life can be traced back to seemingly small events, which started the chain reaction. So never underestimate the potential of taking initiative and embracing new experiences because you never know which horizons it can open.

Summary

- Get involved in activities and initiatives to entertain yourself and grow.

- Try to find systematic problems in the company that affect you to solve them, and create a win-win relationship with your company.

- **Participate in Side Activities**: Reading technical blogs/
  articles, undertaking online courses, participating
  in coding challenges, contributing to open source
  projects, writing technical blogs, mentoring others,
  building personal projects, networking, listening to
  podcasts, reading books, documenting your work,
  participating in hackathons, giving tech talks, getting
  involved in the interview process, and participating or
  organizing an R&D team.

- **Embrace Unexpected Results**: Every non-
  programming activity or initiative has the potential to
  yield unexpected but remarkable results. It's all about
  the cumulative effect of small actions over time.

Reference

[1]   www.researchgate.net/publication/38076549_Employability_
and_Personal_Initiative_as_Antecedents_of_Job_Satisfaction

CHAPTER 5

Burnout

Burnout is an overloaded term. I'm sure you've come across many people who casually drop the phrase, "I'm feeling burned out," into a conversation. Some people might equate it with feeling tired or having a rough week at work. Feeling burnout is not merely being tired because simply working less doesn't solve the problem. It's not having a bad week at work here and there either because burnout doesn't go away on its own after the week. While burnout is not a medical term per se, we should still have a clear definition. So, what exactly is burnout?

According to this resource [1], the primary signs of burnout include persistent fatigue, feelings of helplessness or being trapped, detachment or a sense of isolation, a cynical or negative outlook, self-doubt, procrastination, and a consistent feeling of being overwhelmed. A definition that I like in particular is mentioned by Eric Barker. In a thoughtful blog post on the topic, Eric Barker describes burnout as "a mix of exhaustion, cynicism, and inefficacy. And it feels a lot like depression" [2]. The comparison to depression is particularly insightful. It suggests that we need to address burnout systematically and take it as seriously as we would any other significant mental health concern. However, while depression often makes you lose interest and joy in activities you once enjoyed, burnout doesn't really do that, so there are some distinct differences. You can check out this guide for a more detailed comparison [3].

Before the COVID-19 pandemic, approximately 38% of workers reported experiencing burnout. In the wake of COVID-19, that number rose to 43% [4]. As for software engineers, the situation is even more

© Mykyta Chernenko 2023
M. Chernenko, *The Rational Software Engineer*,
https://doi.org/10.1007/978-1-4842-9795-7_5

challenging. During the pandemic, 54% of software engineers reported feeling burnout to a significant or moderate extent [5]. The primary contributors to this trend were high workloads (reported by 47% of those surveyed), inefficient processes (31%), and unclear goals or targets (29%).

In summary, burnout is a widespread issue, and its prevalence has increased during the COVID-19 era, particularly in remote work environments. As software engineers, we are not immune. Before we address the big signs of burnout, let's take a step back and look at more subtle signals that something is going wrong

Early Red Flags
You Need a Vacation

The idea might raise a few eyebrows, but I believe that if you're constantly daydreaming about your next vacation just to escape work, it might be a red flag. Don't get me wrong, it's essential to take full advantage of your vacation days, and it's completely natural to look forward to them. However, the issue arises when you return from a break and instantly start fantasizing about the next one, indicating your work rhythm might not be sustainable.

A well-balanced workday in a healthy work environment shouldn't leave you feeling mentally overdrawn. Of course, there will be ups and downs, easier weeks, and tougher ones. But consider this: if you had to replicate a typical day at your work for a year without any vacation, do you think your mental state would remain stable? If that sounds like a disaster waiting to happen, it is a bad sign.

You Don't Feel That Your Job Is "Play"

Software engineering is a lot like solving a bunch of little puzzles. It's like those moments when you're solving problems on sites like LeetCode. You crack one, and you can't wait to jump onto the next. That's what most days feel like for me—a fun game that I'm totally into.

But sometimes this playful vibe stops and the fun disappears. It's a very elusive state, but when I see that it has completely vanished and doesn't seem to be coming back, I take it as a warning sign. Something's up.

You Are Becoming Cynical

I tend to deeply care about my job. But it is both a blessing and a curse. On one hand, it drives me and fills me with joy when things go well. On the other hand, research shows that people who care deeply about their jobs are more prone to burnout [6]. That's why it's crucial for me to recognize the early signs. A clear one is when I find myself caring less, changing less, and engaging less. I essentially become more passive and cynical. If I catch myself thinking, "I don't really care," it's a huge sign.

And now, let's address common burnout causes and how to deal with them.

Causes

High Workload

I personally feel that staying late at work fixing some critical issue or brushing up on a feature that you want to complete is pretty much fun if it is done sporadically and the environment is not pushing. On the contrary, being in a situation where staying late is an environmental habit or having permanent upcoming deadlines, extra important throw-everything-you-do-now-and-fix-this production bug, or having higher performance expectations that one can achieve is detrimental.

So when I notice that having a high workload is a constant state of my work, I know I need to fix it because I borrow from my resource pool, and if it is going to continue for a while, my pool will end up empty. And it is going to punch me back in my face. Hard.

This is often an issue that must be addressed with your manager as they can typically solve it, tell you when it can be solved, or explain why it cannot be solved at all—the case when you understand that you have other options open in front of you.

Once I was working in a startup that had a tight budget, and last-minute changes, overtime, and a high workload were the norm. When we asked the manager for the strategy to deal with that, he said that it's the nature of the company to execute it in such a way. "We are a startup!" It made me clear that if I want to stay sane, I should not linger on the project for a long time. My mental stability is much more important to me than continuously meeting deadlines with vague benefits.

For the startup, their execution was a sprinting, win-or-die situation because they needed to secure another financing round and were always running out of money. But for me my job is a marathon—I need to think about me remaining stable and passionate through my long career. I don't want to overperform for six months and try to deal with the consequences of burnout for another year. I didn't have to leave them as I got reassigned to another project and the company closed soon anyway, but I knew that it would be my choice as well.

Typically, a high workload can be solved by

- Constraining it in a time period so that you have short bouts of overtime

- Putting/hiring more resources to distribute the load

- Reducing the performance expectations so that it's not expected you will work overtime

Also, I've seen behavior that is more typical for junior software engineers—to prove that you are a great developer to somebody else by working much more than required. It can come from fear of being fired or from feeling insecure because you produce less code than other more experienced colleagues. The truth is that it is expected that it will take more time and some guidance to achieve the same result as for more senior peers. Be careful of somebody who would utilize your junior title as an excuse for you to work more. You don't have to.

Inefficient Processes

Inefficient processes can be both time-consuming and frustrating. Imagine if you have a gatekeeper security manager who is the only one who has access to the company DNS provider. And to add a new subdomain, which is a fairly frequent process, you need to create a ticket, wait for her for a week to pick it up, and schedule a call, and then she doubts all of the actions you do even though she personally does not know how to configure DNS records. Or that you want to change the blur of the background picture by 10% and do A/B testing, but to do that, you need to submit a formal design change proposal document and get approval from the design committee in the company. Or that you must write a 200-word review to 20 engineers in your department every half a year even though you work only with two colleagues all the time.

Some bad processes are created as failed experiments, some are residues from different company times, some are cargo cults, and some are improvements of even worse processes.

As I mentioned in Chapter 4, "Initiative," it is good to try to change such things. It happened to me a lot of times that I would propose to change how we organize meetings or ask to cancel it altogether or I would explain how terrible or frustrating some process feels and how I see it becoming better. At times I got a decent explanation of why things are like that, at times the processes were changed, and at times nothing happened at all, and I needed to bear with that. But I knew that I tried what was in my power.

Unclear Goals and Targets

This thing kills even the strongest. I think you've seen the folks who have no idea why they develop some piece of software or why they are kept in the office as well. With losing the goal, one loses the sense of meaning. This is why it is so important to align the whole team on the goals and explain why they do the things they do. When I see the whole picture, it inspires me because now I know what I contribute to and how to do it. Essentially, if you have no goals, you feel no meaning, no impact, and no value.

Most often I see the absence of clear goals on a project due to three things:

- Poor team communication so that the goals are not shared efficiently or kept in silos

- Sunset of the team because the project is doomed

- Absence of a good product manager who will find the goal, which ultimately leads to the previous point

If there is no clear goal for a team and the team does not understand why they exist, it leads to the imminent sunset of the team because, well, it's a pricey team of developers not put to work. In such situations, I try to reach the management to understand how I can be useful elsewhere. If it is not possible, I know that I need to look for another job.

When there is no clear goal, I tend to become cynical. I try to dissociate from the company, and I become disinterested in what it wants to accomplish because I cannot contribute to that. This is why I find having a clear goal in the company to be so important.

Lack of Community

Friends are essential, not only in our personal lives but also in our work environment. Research by Gallup suggests that having a best friend at work is closely tied to positive business outcomes, such as better profitability, safety, inventory control, and improved employee retention [7]. A global study by the International Social Survey Program (ISSP) has shown that interpersonal relationships at work significantly enhance job satisfaction [8]. Moreover, having at least one friend at work can make you 96% more likely to be satisfied with your life [9].

I've had the privilege of having friends join me at my workplace and also forming new friendships while on the job. There were times when my friends joined the same company as me, and we ended up collaborating on the same project. I still remember that time as one of the funniest couple of moments in my career. Brainstorming together, designing the system, and backing each other up all felt like a game when done with my friend. Before, we used to team up to solve tasks together and discuss work-related things just because it was nice to do it with a friend. But that time we also got paid for that, which made it the perfect working condition. I feel the same vibe when my wife and I brainstorm solutions and ideas for my startup. I enjoy being with her; I enjoy working on my startup, and combining it doubles the effect. Unfortunately, as great as it is, it is rarely possible to bring your best pals to your daily duties. But the good part is that it is possible to foster this vibe by creating deeper connections at work and making friends there.

It's always beneficial to interact with a good number of people from your company to make it happen; chances are, you'll find someone you click with and can enjoy being in the same room. While people might not readily open up at the workplace, they are often more willing to engage during lunch breaks or after-work events. Here are some tips to create workplace friendships:

- **Mix It Up at Lunchtime**: When you join a new company, try to have lunch with different colleagues instead of sticking only with your team or eating alone.

- **Connect Outside of Work**: Invite colleagues to events they might find interesting, and make an effort to join them.

- **Participate in Company Events**: Take part in or organize "random coffee" events at your workplace, which can provide an informal setting to interact with your colleagues.

- **Bring Your Friends on Board**: If you have friends looking for opportunities, invite them to join your company. It's a win-win as it helps your company and enriches your work life.

Lack of Change

Once in my youth, I got a chance to work one day at a steel tools factory, where I needed to help throw away some old equipment from a warehouse. Even though it was pretty dynamic to me as we fooled around and talked during the whole time with my friend, I also noticed how repetitive were the tasks the employees performed themselves. I cannot erase the memory of a guy pressing down a lever every 15 seconds and after that waiting for another 15 seconds to do it again with a vacant look. I haven't ever seen a deeper absence of meaning than in his eyes. At that moment I decided that I would never want to have a job where I'd need to do similar things over and over again.

Even though I will likely never be able to experience the emptiness that guy did, when I am tasked with similar things, I start getting frustrated. Repetition, no matter how enjoyable the task, can eventually lead to boredom. This is why diversification in our activities, automatization, and learning are so crucial, as well as seeking novelty and a high level of experiments in the career in general.

Lack of Control

If we're only given instructions with no room for personal input or responsibility, it can be demotivating quickly. Some workplaces have this as part of their culture, which is difficult to change. However, if it's only one or two individuals in the team who are taking away control and responsibility from others, it's worth having a conversation with them to express your concerns.

There's a significant difference between shielding employees from being overwhelmed with changes and external influences and telling them exactly what to do. A good manager knows how to protect their team from excessive information and uncertainty while still providing them with the freedom to make decisions and have an impact.

In essence, employees need to feel empowered. They need to be allowed to take charge of their work, make decisions, and contribute ideas. This not only fosters a sense of ownership and responsibility but also boosts morale and job satisfaction. It's about finding the right balance between providing guidance and giving autonomy, and it's a crucial part of creating a healthy and motivating work environment.

Lack of Values

Working for a company that doesn't align with your values can lead to problems. You might always feel something is wrong, and you could become negative or cynical over time. For example, if you care about health and wellness, it could feel wrong to work for a company that sells tobacco products. Our values are something that stays with us for a long time, sometimes forever, and the same is true for companies. So, if there's a mismatch, it can't easily be fixed.

That's why it's important to know your own values before you start job hunting. You should try to find a company that shares those values. We'll talk more about this later.

Distress

Light levels of stress can be beneficial [10] [11]. This type of stress, often referred to as eustress, can create manageable challenges, push us beyond our comfort zones in a safe setting, or provide realistic deadlines that keep us on track. For example, as I write this book, I experience a mild level of stress due to the looming deadline. It's not overly tight, but it's also not a walk in the park. This encourages me to maintain my focus and prioritize my writing.

On the contrary, excessive stress, or distress, is harmful. It's a classic "lose-lose" scenario in the job context for both you and your employer as it diminishes your performance and job satisfaction over time. Therefore, a proficient manager will always strive to mitigate distress.

Interestingly, when I began writing this book, I felt more anxious about the deadline, which led me to overwork, negatively affecting my sleep and overall mood. I knew that if I continued on this path, it would lead to a less-than-desirable outcome. Consequently, I had to reassess my plan, set an upper limit on my weekly writing hours, and commit to only writing when I found it enjoyable. Eventually, I learned to rest without feeling the urge to write, which helped me transition from distress to eustress.

One of the common stressors at work is the fear of running out of time. Many people become anxious if they can't complete a task within the estimated time frame, leading to excessive overtime to meet the "deadline." Funny that, these deadlines are often self-imposed. Most of our work comes with an estimate, not a hard commitment. An estimate is an educated guess of the time required, which could end up being more or less than anticipated. There's no shame in missing an estimate, and it is common knowledge that estimates are not precise. Over time, work should roughly align with these estimates, and if it doesn't, it will simply indicate your tendency to underestimate or overestimate tasks.

If strict deadlines are indeed a part of your role, ensure they are realistic. A competent manager will work with you to adjust deadlines accordingly, so you can avoid distress.

In case of persistent stress issues, consider other stress management tools such as meditation, deep rest techniques, breathing exercises, physical activities, or psychotherapy.

What If I Have Burnout Already?

If you're reading this and you're experiencing burnout, I want to say I'm sorry you're going through this. I understand it's a tough situation and it may feel like there's no way out. But recovery is absolutely possible, and it's within your control.

First, you need to identify what's causing your burnout. It could be one of the factors we've discussed or something unique to your situation. Writing these down can be a helpful starting point.

Next, consider which of these factors can be changed at your current job. Perhaps there's one particular issue that's causing a lot of trouble. For example, you might be facing extremely tight deadlines, or there could be a specific work process that's causing you distress.

Then, try to make those changes. It might feel daunting, especially when you're already feeling low on energy, but imagine how much better things could be if the sources of your burnout were removed. Wouldn't it be worth the effort to try and make that happen?

Talk to your manager or even their manager. Be open and honest about how you're feeling, what you believe the issues are, and any potential solutions you can think of. Don't be afraid to say you might leave if things don't change. Your honesty could trigger some significant changes. Once again, employers can do a lot for valuable employees.

However, there might be situations where change didn't happen or is not possible, for instance, when your personal values don't align with the company's. In these cases, it's best to leave as quickly as possible for the sake of your well-being. It might be scary, but there's no point in prolonging a miserable situation when you have the power to find happiness elsewhere.

Summary

- Be aware of early warning signs leading to burnout: feeling like you need a vacation, the work stops feeling like a "play," and you start becoming cynical.

- Recognize symptoms of burnout such as constant tiredness, loss of motivation, fatigue, and feelings of helplessness.

- Avoid prolonged periods of high workload. If necessary, discuss this with your manager and find ways to manage it better.

- Aim to identify and improve inefficient processes within your company.

- Ensure that you and your team have clear goals to work toward.

- Seek out a workplace that aligns with your personal values.

- Keep your role interesting by learning new things and taking on new tasks.

- Make sure you have some level of autonomy and decision-making power in your role.

- Prioritize your physical and mental health.

- If you're already experiencing burnout, identify the cause, and attempt to change it. If change isn't possible in your current job, it might be time to look for a new one.

References

[1] https://mentalhealth-uk.org/burnout/

[2] https://bakadesuyo.com/2023/04/burnout/

[3] www.nytimes.com/2022/08/23/well/mind/burnout-depression-symptoms-treatment.html

[4] www.weforum.org/agenda/2021/12/employees-stress-mental-health-workplace-environment/#:~:text=43%25%20of%20respondents%20in%20over,daily%20stress%20globally%20at%2057%25

[5] https://haystack-books.s3.amazonaws.com/Study+to+understand+the+impact+of+COVID-19+on+Software+Engineers+-+Full+Report.pdf

[6] www.davewhiteside.com/anatomyofapurposedrivenemployee

[7] The Increasing Importance of a Best Friend at Work (gallup.com)

[8] https://search.gesis.org/research_data/ZA6770

[9] www.amazon.co.uk/dp/0063050943?tag=baupthwrtr-21&geniuslink=true

[10] Researchers find out why some stress is good for you | Berkeley News

[11] Good Stress, Bad Stress and Oxidative Stress: Insights from Anticipatory Cortisol Reactivity - PMC (nih.gov)

CHAPTER 6

What to Avoid in the Long Run

There are many decisions that might seem like a good choice in the short run. We've already covered one of these—procrastination. It might seem like a good idea at the moment, but if you consider it from a long-term perspective, it's clearly counterproductive. The best practice is to reflect on where a certain decision will lead you if you continue in the same way for an extended period. Will it contribute to your growth, or will it cause you to stagnate? In this chapter, I will discuss a few such behaviors that are best avoided as they constitute self-sabotaging behaviors.

Not Engaging in Hard Things

Sometimes, we avoid things for good reasons. Fear and anxiety can be rational responses. Let's say you dodge leading a software engineering department because you have absolutely no experience managing people. Or, you refuse a tight deadline because it feels unrealistic. This kind of avoidance makes sense. But, there are other tough choices we should face, even if they seem hard.

Imagine you're uneasy about being in the spotlight, even with just a few people around. So, you steer clear from it, thinking, "I'm not the public-speaking type." That might feel like the right call, but in reality, you're limiting yourself. You're closing doors on opportunities like

© Mykyta Chernenko 2023
M. Chernenko, *The Rational Software Engineer*,
https://doi.org/10.1007/978-1-4842-9795-7_6

effectively explaining your design document to a group of peers, speaking at local conferences, or leading a large team. You might not see it now, but if you look further, you'll realize how many things become out of reach just because you're not facing your fear.

Those relaxed folks you see on stage didn't just wake up one day and start speaking confidently. They were scared at first. They may still feel scared. I don't know anyone who finds public speaking a breeze. Even seasoned speakers have some level of anxiety from time to time. They had to train and grow to get there and still need to push to perform on the stage.

So if you're brave enough to step into a task in a slightly challenging environment, you'll see progress. You might start by giving a talk to your team, then to multiple teams, then lead a meeting, and eventually, you could be presenting to the whole company or even comfortably speaking at a conference.

And this isn't just a made-up story. I have social anxiety. Talking to a group of people, especially when presenting, is tough for me. I remember how intense was the blushing, the mind fog, and the far-from-relaxed behavior. But I've gone from struggling with one-on-one chats to performing on stage, pitching to large crowds, and giving company-wide talks. It took years, and I'm far from perfect at it, but I can do it when necessary. And when I look back, I see a huge difference. My approach was to consistently tackle tasks that felt scary but manageable, a six out of ten in terms of fear. I practiced until I became comfortable, then moved on to a slightly harder task that would now also feel six out of ten. So it should not be overwhelming, but it must be always challenging. This method is essentially exposure therapy, a proven way to handle similar anxieties and deal with irrational fear in general [1].

My general rule is this: If something feels out of my comfort zone, scary, or difficult, I need to dig deeper into it. More often than not, fear is a good indicator of an area that I need to develop myself in, and by overcoming it, I can become a better specialist.

Manual Work

Manual work typically isn't appealing, especially for us engineers who specialize in automating manual tasks. Many engineers I know tend to automate more rather than less. However, that wasn't my approach initially.

I used to be very pragmatic about what I would automate. If a process took ten minutes every month, but automating it would take half a day, I'd usually opt not to automate it due to the upfront time cost.

However, recently, I got a task with which my approach led me to deep frustration, so my stance had to change. I had to convert a repetitive and complex JSON structure into a set of in-code objects using our types and our in-house templating library. The task was daunting and time-consuming. It seemed that automating it would take even longer due to the numerous steps involved, so I opted to do it manually.

I estimated that it would take me two weeks to complete half of the task manually. Throughout this period, I found myself procrastinating and dreading the task. I took on other tasks to avoid it and tried to bargain with myself. As a result, it took me a month to produce the output that should've taken two weeks, and it didn't feel great.

As I still had half of the file left to process, I realized that it might make more sense to spend three weeks automating the task rather than suffering through the manual work that I disliked. And those three weeks of coding were far more enjoyable.

Did I theoretically spend more time on automation? Yes. But in reality, I doubt I would have completed the manual task in two weeks because I found it so disappointing. More importantly, the automation process was engaging and enjoyable. I didn't have to force myself through it and didn't procrastinate.

Since then, I've started counting the mental cost of lengthy manual tasks when deciding whether to automate them. This approach allows me to compare the true costs of manual work and automation more fairly.

Victim Mindset

I've alluded to the victim mindset before, emphasizing that we always have the power to change almost any job situation. The methods may vary, but the ability to influence our circumstances is always there.

I've seen some software engineers stuck in the same stagnating job for years, unhappy with their conditions, and met people who constantly complain about their colleagues without ever trying to approach them for a constructive conversation. Small behaviors where we play the victim can easily start a negative spiral, eventually leading to a state of learned helplessness.

The concept of learned helplessness was initially studied in the 1960s in experiments involving dogs conditioned to expect pain or suffering without a way to escape [2]. Researchers observed that dogs who were repeatedly exposed to unavoidable shocks eventually stopped trying to escape, even when they were put in situations where escape was possible. This contrasted sharply with a control group of dogs that always tried to escape when they were given the means to do so. When this concept was later applied to human psychology, it was found that individuals' motivation can significantly decrease when they perceive a loss of control over a situation. This diminished motivation can persist even after circumstances change.

When I find myself behaving as a victim, I recognize it as self-sabotaging behavior because it's not the state I want to be in. If I'm complaining about something and I haven't tried to change it, why am I complaining? I am trying to focus on a small change that I can do just to break a circle and get back on track. Maybe a good first step is to drop a message to somebody you need to talk with or even simply write a new point in your to-do list that will be a reminder that you need to do something when you have a little bit more energy.

A related issue is feeling as though you can't leave your job because you'd be betraying your company or colleagues. You might feel as though you "owe" them because they gave you your first job or because a mentor at your workplace has invested a lot of time in you. While fairness is important, it's also crucial to remember that there's nothing worse than suffering in your workplace, which not only affects you but also those around you who have to deal with an unmotivated, frustrated colleague. If your company tries to make you feel guilty about leaving, then this is pure manipulation, a red flag that makes the decision to leave even clearer.

Difficult Discussions

One of the typical difficult discussions a lot of people avoid is 1:1s. However, 1:1s are a great tool to stay in sync with your manager and the company, exchange feedback, and get direction, among other things. According to Gullup employees who have regular 1:1 meetings with their managers are 3x (!) more likely to be engaged at work [3]. Despite their many benefits, 1:1s can be emotionally challenging. They require vulnerability as you expose your fears, and there's always a level of uncertainty about how the other person will respond. This is why it's so easy to simply avoid 1:1s. It's easy to find reasons to skip these meetings due to busyness, and before you know it, weeks have turned into months without a 1:1.

If you find yourself in such a position, try to get back on track and make 1:1s a habit. If you continually find yourself skipping these meetings, aim to schedule them at least once a month and make a point to keep them regularly.

Isolating Yourself

Sometimes, I realize I don't want to be in the office as much, or I'm not as eager to join a brainstorming session or a get-together after work. This can gradually make me feel distant from the team, and it basically shows signs of me being unhappy with the other team members, how we collaborate, or our work in general. Whether it's a colleague I don't get along with, a stressful atmosphere, or face-to-face teamwork that isn't effective, I know that avoiding the office work and keeping to myself usually isn't a good plan and it can cause problems later.

You Start Slacking Off

It might be tempting to cut back on your work hours a bit in an effort to recharge and improve your mental health. However, if I find myself taking a sick leave when I'm not that ill, or wanting to leave work early, I see it as a potential warning sign. When I'm passionate about what I do, I feel disappointed if I get sick, and I also don't find myself constantly checking the clock to leave because I enjoy my work. So, if that changes, I start thinking about what I can adjust.

Self-Sabotaging Behaviors

The typical behaviors mentioned earlier aren't the only self-sabotaging behaviors we engage in. Each one of us has it in some way or another. Perhaps you know you need to brush up on your knowledge, but you keep delaying it by weeks, or you know that you need to request a project change, but you avoid scheduling the meeting. Maybe you are aware that notifications on your phone are hampering your productivity, yet you still don't turn them off. Sometimes it is much harder to deal with these behaviors because they are not purely productivity issues. We're not ignorant; we know it's not helpful to browse social media as our deadline looms, but we still do it. And sometimes it indicates an unresolved emotional issue.

That's why it is sometimes important to step back and try to identify a broader problem instead of focusing solely on the small behavior at hand. For example, as I am from Ukraine, I find it hard not to check news updates every day, writing it in 2023. As unhelpful as I find this behavior to be, I just can't help myself. For me, this is a seek to calm myself and feel that I am in control, so I let it be. Fortunately, this habit doesn't consume much time, but simply acknowledging that there can sometimes be a larger issue behind a small behavior helps to stop self-blame and encourages a more pragmatic approach to the issue.

Summary

- **Engage in Challenging Tasks**: Start with smaller tasks that seem a little out of your comfort zone and gradually take on bigger ones.

- **Consider Automation**: Even if a task takes a short time to complete manually, the mental cost can be high. Consider automating repetitive tasks, not just to save time but also to reduce mental fatigue and procrastination.

- **Avoid the Victim Mindset**: Try not to fall into a negative spiral of victimhood and learned helplessness by doing a small change.

- **Establish Regular 1:1 Meetings**: Make it a habit.

- **Identify and Address Self-Sabotaging Behaviors**: If you notice a behavior that's counterproductive, try to understand the underlying issues and address or accept them.

References

[1]   https://ebbp.org/resources/Anxiety_Exposure
       TherapyandCBT_FAQ.pdf

[2]   www.ncbi.nlm.nih.gov/pmc/articles/PMC4920136/

[3]   www.gallup.com/workplace/236450/managers-millennials-
       feedback-won-ask.aspx

CHAPTER 7

Career Change

Having long-term career goals is useful. They act as a guiding North Star in our career journey, enabling us to periodically assess if we're heading in the right direction. For many professionals, especially those in senior roles, setting dramatically different career goals can be challenging. I know several individuals who, after five to ten years, have reached senior or staff software engineer positions and are content with continuing in that role. They have no desire to transition into solution architects, tech leads, or CTO roles; their passion lies in development.

Yet, even when one wishes to continue being in the same role, there still can be a long-term goal. It might be a desire to join a specific company, work on a distinct project, or delve deeper into a specialized domain. And short-term goals can always be effectively employed as well. There are always milestones to strive for within a year. I make it a point to outline a list of objectives I wish to accomplish within the year, including professional ones, early in January. To fully leverage this practice, it's advisable to set SMART goals.

SMART is an acronym for specific, measurable, achievable, relevant, and time-bound goals. Here's an explanation of what each term signifies:

- **Specific**: Goals should be clear, concise, and specific, not ambiguous or broad. They should answer: What do I want to achieve? Why is this goal important? Who is involved?

© Mykyta Chernenko 2023
M. Chernenko, *The Rational Software Engineer*,
https://doi.org/10.1007/978-1-4842-9795-7_7

- **Measurable**: Goals should have specific criteria for measuring the progress. This helps in monitoring your advancement and maintaining motivation. It answers: How will I know when it's accomplished?

- **Achievable**: Goals should be realistic and attainable, not far-fetched and improbable. They should challenge your abilities but remain within reach. It answers: How can I accomplish this goal?

- **Relevant**: Goals should align with your life and career. They should be consistent with your other goals and values. It answers: Is this worthwhile, and does it align with my other efforts?

- **Time-Bound**: Goals should have a deadline to foster a sense of urgency and facilitate progress tracking. It answers: When will I accomplish this goal?

Let's compare a SMART goal with a non-SMART goal:

"I want to get better at programming." What does "better" mean? How will you measure your progress? When will you assess your success?

"I want to read three professional books within a year." This goal clearly defines what to do, how to measure progress halfway through, and when to evaluate success or failure.

If you are curious to see what my list of yearly goals looks like, here it is:

- Read five professional books.

- Deliver a public speech at a technical conference.

- ~~Attract 100 monthly users to the Nemlys app~~

- Add one more team member.

- Transition to a consultancy role if it is a safe choice.

- Spend five hours in focused work for at least 180 days.

- Complete a hands-on hacker course.

- Finish the architecture track on roadmap.sh.

- ~~Offer free mentorship to one individual from Ukraine~~

While some goals align perfectly with the SMART framework, others can be somewhat challenging to confine within these boundaries, but you get the gist.

Now, what if, even with clear goals, you still feel stuck? Or you want to make a big change but you're not sure what it is or how to go about it?

Feeling Stuck

At certain points in our lives, feeling stuck is inevitable. This is a normal experience. Research even indicates a pattern to this feeling; we often question existential aspects of our lives roughly every decade, starting from the age of 29 [1]. This cycle, where we feel lost, reflect on things, make changes, and then launch into a new phase of personal development, is an unavoidable part of life.

And I definitely can relate to feeling stuck. When I started my journey as a Python developer, I was enthusiastic about the limitless potential of using Python and Django in web development. I also dabbled in JavaScript and Vue/React for some front-end work, constantly intrigued and stimulated by the new concepts I was learning. However, over time, I started feeling stagnant. The technologies I was utilizing didn't excite me as before, and the tasks seemed monotonous and unchallenging. I found myself delving into the depth of documentation to learn something novel in my main area of focus, but it no longer had a significant influence on my code.

During that period, I was wrestling with numerous questions: "Should I continue with Python? Is back-end development still the right choice for me? Should I even persist with software engineering?"

I was longing for a change but was filled with uncertainty about my next steps. I know many others have experienced similar feelings, which can be demotivating and daunting. But I firmly believe that such moments can also offer the most life-changing opportunities.

Do I Want to Be a Software Engineer at All?

First, I asked myself ground questions to see if I wanted to stay in this field at all.

These questions are similar to the idea of Ikigai—a Japanese concept meaning "a reason for being." As shown in Figure 7-1, Ikigai says that the best job is something you love, you're good at, and the world needs, and will pay you enough for. So I asked myself, "Does programming fit into all these categories?"

Figure 7-1. *Ikigai*

For me, the answer was clear "YES!" I felt like it was the perfect fit for me, so I didn't think about changing fields. But I know not everyone feels the same. I've seen people who joined the tech field for the money and job security, but they didn't really like the work. Being a software engineer can seem like a great job, but it's not for everyone. You can learn to be good at something, but it's hard to learn to love it.

Big and Scary Career Change

So what if you indeed decided on a major career change, for example, that software engineering doesn't drive you and you want to go into marketing? You have several options to make this shift easier:

- Gradually move into the new role at your current job.

- Keep your job while learning about the new field in your free time.

- Go all in, quit your current job, and focus on breaking into the new industry.

The first option is great if you can do it. You'd transition while still doing some of your old job. Suppose you want to move into marketing. If your company has a good marketing team, you might be able to start taking on some of their tasks. You'd gain experience as you learn, and you'd probably keep most of your current pay. I tried this approach when I was interested in product management. It felt like I could have made the full switch if I had decided to.

The second option works well if the new field is quite different from your current one. You'd keep your regular pay while learning new skills at your own pace. You might read books on the topic, take a course, or start a project in a new field. You can do this with just a few hours each week, and it can be enough to help you find a new job. The downsides? It can take longer to switch, and you might find it hard to learn after a long day at work. When you do switch, you might have to take a pay cut because the experience you gain in this way isn't usually seen as "work" experience.

The last option is to go all in. You'd quit your current job and focus entirely on learning and finding a new job. This option can be exciting if you have enough savings or if you can manage without an income for a few months. You'd have plenty of time to learn, and the need to find a new job could be a powerful motivator. And let's not forget the added motivation in finding a new job because, well, you don't have any other option now. :)

Making big changes can be scary and tough. But if you're moving into a field you're really passionate about, it's totally worth it. You can often see a difference in happiness between people who enjoy their work and those who don't.

Now, let's go back to my situation and the questions I asked myself.

Management

As you gain more experience, managing tasks becomes part of the job. For a skilled engineer, it can be tempting to move into a managerial role. But remember, being a great software engineer doesn't mean you'll be a great tech lead, project manager, or in any role where you deal with clients. I've seen many excellent engineers move into management and lose touch with what they're really good at—coding.

Let's be real, talented engineers don't always make the best managers. Our field is full of top-notch engineers who became managers and then think their main job is to be the best tech expert or even the smartest person in the room. That can make them mediocre or even bad managers.

At the same time, there is tremendous value in a good manager. There are specific traits and behaviors that make a great manager. They should be an "enabler" for their team. That means they need to be good at dealing with people and be deeply empathetic. They also need to know how to build good communication and foster a supportive vibe. I've seen people who naturally create the right atmosphere in their team. They motivate others to learn and grow, they cheer up their teammates when needed, they express gratitude and admiration when they feel it, they stand up for the team when it's right, and they make the team feel safe. They know when to say "sorry" and "thank you." This set of traits is rare in the technical field, but those who have them and grow into managers create great things, and people mention them with kind words years after. If you recognize yourself in the text or you are willing to change to get there, I personally beg you: grow into a manager.

As for me, I wasn't sure. The idea of managing people and helping them grow sounded good. But I needed to try it out before deciding. I kept that option open and waited for the right time to give it a go. As of now, I realize that managing for me takes more energy than it gives, and I know that I'm not a great people manager.

Shifting My Focus from the Back End

There were a lot of shiny subfields out there: front end, data science, data engineering, DevOps, mobile development, game development, you name it. I wanted to understand whether I would enjoy myself more in another specialization.

After exploring some of the technologies myself and asking other people, I realized that back end is still something that I like doing as it has one of the shortest feedback loops I've seen in development. When I have a task, I am typically able to break it down to a microtask, which takes me 5–20 minutes to code, and then I can typically run test it in a matter of one minute. It makes the experience very pleasant and almost gamelike.

T-Shaped Development

Another choice was to remain primarily a Python back-end developer but broaden my skills with more technologies. Often, a good combo would be to add more front-end knowledge. I've noticed that fullstack developers are typically rather T-shaped developers, having deep expertise in either front end or back end, with some knowledge across the other. So this way, I could keep doing the work I'm good at and enjoy while expanding my skills on the side. I found this idea appealing, and I believe it's a good move toward becoming a versatile software engineer if that's what someone wants.

Software Engineering in a Broader Sense

To me, the ideal software engineer is like a one-person band. They use the right tools to solve business problems from start to finish. They set up the project, collect data, develop, style, and deploy it. It's hard to be an expert at everything, but such engineers get a broad overview and a wide range of concepts to work with.

This option appealed to me. It meant using a broad set of technologies, continually learning, and getting satisfaction from handling all tasks from beginning to end.

What Did I End Up With?

I was a Python developer. I decided to broaden my skills by adding front end to my stack, becoming a T-shaped developer and eventually a software engineer, while keeping a preference for back end. I also chose to take on more side tasks and be open to a managerial role.

Ask People

There are always plenty of career options to take. One strategy that is useful for any kind of career change is to ask people who work in the relevant fields. Often, a lot of doubts can be cleared out if you find two to five people who work with the new shiny thing you want to work with and ask them what they like about it and don't. You can ask your friends/colleagues to introduce you to somebody or reach out to 50 people on LinkedIn who resemble your path (live in the same city, have similar years of experience, and come from the same cultural background) and ask those who accept your request a few questions. A lot of people are really nice out there and will gladly help you and share their experiences. I didn't initially realize, for example, that to evaluate accuracy in machine learning, you typically need to wait hours for your model to train, which makes the feedback loop tremendously long.

I like asking the following questions:

- What do you like the most about what you do?

- Are there any things that you do not find exciting but you must do anyway?

- What is the ideal position in your field for you and how realistic is it to get there?

- How was your experience the last time you changed your job?

Summary

- Use long-term or short-term goals to guide your progress.

- If you feel the need for a career change, first ask yourself if software engineering is still something you love, are good at, and can earn enough from and if it's something the world needs. This can help you decide whether to stay in the field or switch.

- If you decide to completely switch fields, consider these options:

  - Gradually shift into the new role within your current workplace if possible.

  - Keep your current job while gaining experience and knowledge in the new field in your spare time.

  - Take the leap and fully commit to breaking into the new industry

- If you're making a more subtle change, do the following:

  - Get hands-on experience with the things you want to transition to.

  - Understand which style suits you better: specialist developer (like a Python developer), T-shaped developer, or software engineer.

  - Consider managerial tasks.

- Connect with other professionals in the area you want to move into and ask them questions.

Last but not least, if you ever decide on a job change—good luck! I hope your transition goes smoothly and is an exciting experience!

Reference

[1]   https://pubmed.ncbi.nlm.nih.gov/25404347/

CHAPTER 8

How to Find a Dream Job

So, you're at a point where you're not happy with your current job. It could be that you can't see yourself growing as a software engineer or your company's values don't fit with yours. Maybe your project isn't what you hoped for, and you can't change it, or you're missing things like a good work-life balance, nice relationships with colleagues, or a fair salary. Or, you could be in an even better place: you don't need to get a new job right now, you're just keeping your eyes open.

Searching for a new position can be exciting, but at the same time, the hiring process can be long and frustrating, and it's easy to make a mistake and pick the wrong company. So, is there something you can do to make the hiring process as nice as possible and find a great new job? Yes, there are quite a few helpful tips.

Before we start, one thing I need to make clear is that some of the advice here is more applicable when you are in such a place in your career where the companies are "hunting" for you, not the other way around. This is usually the case for most software engineers with at least a couple of years of experience when the market is in your favor. But it can be very different if you're looking for your first job or the market is in a "crisis" state, like during the start of the COVID-19 time or during the massive layoffs in 2022. In cases like that, it might be smarter to be more agreeable and less picky.

Let's start with the "preparation" phase.

M. Chernenko, *The Rational Software Engineer*,
https://doi.org/10.1007/978-1-4842-9795-7_8

Try to Be Not in a Hurry

The best time to start looking for a new job is when you don't have any pressure to find one quickly. If you have to get a new job fast, it will limit your choices and how much you're willing to compromise. Being able to say no is a powerful tool. Knowing that you can just stay in your current job if the new one isn't perfect gives you a lot of control. If there's a part of the contract you don't agree with or they don't agree with your counteroffer, and the company threatens to withdraw the offer, well, that's their loss. If you can't get the exact salary you want, or you're not sure about a company, you don't have to take the risk. I can't stress enough how beneficial it is to start job hunting well in advance and always be passively looking for opportunities.

Some chances pop up out of the blue. It's not likely that the company you've got your eye on will have the exact job you want when you start your job hunt. For example, I'm really interested in neurobiology, and I've been trying to find a job as a software engineer in the field for a while. There might be only a few hundred of those jobs in the world each year. So I try to check new job postings in selected neuroscience-related companies every couple of months to see if there are any new jobs I should apply for. Even if a job does pop up, it's not a sure thing that I'll get it. But if I do, I will likely take it.

In general, it's helpful to have a list of five to ten companies you fancy especially and to regularly check if they have any new job openings. And if you're looking for a rare position, it's good to keep an eye on when they become available, even in companies you don't know about yet. For example, there might only be a few dozen CTO positions in your city each year, most of them at companies you don't know about yet. You don't want to miss those.

Lots of job search websites have a feature to save your job searches, which I find really helpful. You can sign up to get updates from the companies you're interested in and for the job titles you're looking for, so you can see new opportunities as soon as they come up.

And doing well in interviews is a skill, and you can quickly get rusty if you don't exercise. So it's useful to go for job interviews a few times each year. It will help you to remember how the interviews go, to be most used to and relaxed at them, and even more importantly, show you whether companies are gradually more interested in you, which they should be if you are gaining experience on a competitive track.

And now let's talk about how to get a job without even getting to an interview

Why Personal References Matter Much

PayScale states [1] that about 70–85% of jobs aren't even advertised. Companies often hire new employees through references and networking. Even if a job is advertised, having a reference can increase your chances of getting hired by about six times. So, how do you find these unadvertised jobs?

Networking is the key. We'll talk about how to broaden your professional network in other chapters. But, for now, here are a few things that are relevant to the job search.

One strategy is to connect with people in the company you're interested in. You can do this in many ways. Maybe the company hosts public events that you can attend. Maybe they have a booth at a conference. You can also reach out directly to someone in the company. You can send a message to an HR or technical employee, telling them you like what their company is doing and you'd like to get to know them better. I've seen multiple people end up like that at our after-hours hangouts. By the time a job opens up, companies already know they are. They might hear about jobs that aren't advertised or be considered as having a reference. This works especially well for small and medium-sized companies.

For larger companies with more structured processes, you could try to meet a few technical employees ahead of time. You could have an informal chat with them or grab a coffee to learn more about the company. If you manage to show your expertise, you could later ask them if they can provide you with a reference in the future process.

Maintaining an active presence on professional social media platforms can also be very helpful. For example, if you're job hunting and you have a thousand connections on LinkedIn, a post saying you're looking for a new opportunity could make a big impact.

Let's now switch to how to show your experience with a good CV.

Brush Up Your CV

If you haven't updated your CV since you started at your last job, now is the time to do so. It's even better to keep updating it regularly even when you're not actively job hunting. I aim to refresh my CV every month or so because it's easy to forget important details, like the challenges I've tackled.

I keep the most important stuff on the first page—my contact details and all the companies I've worked for, outlining my roles, the tech stacks I've used, and key achievements. The second page is dedicated to my worldview and passions as a software engineer, my future goals, the technologies I'm familiar with, and my personal outstanding accomplishments.

Feel free to structure your CV in your own way; there are plenty of good options. My advice would be to make sure the first page has all the essentials as many recruiters will not look at your CV for longer than ten seconds. It's also useful to design your CV so it can be easily processed by recruitment software, which can categorize what you've written.

While making your CV creative or humorous can be tempting, I'd advise against it. It's hard to impress a software engineer with technical skills through an artistic or interactive CV. Usually, your CV will be read by three people: a recruiter, a manager, and a technical person. Most of them won't have the time or inclination to dig deep into a quirky CV. If you want to show your creativity, it's better to keep your CV simple and include a link to your personal interactive website.

Considering that three types of people will read your CV, it's a good idea to seek feedback from each. Find someone who is a recruiter, a manager, and a technical person, and ask if your CV is clear and presents a good overview of you. With your initial version, you're likely to receive some valuable feedback.

It's common in some fields to tweak CVs for each position you apply to. I don't think it's as useful for software engineers since our experience isn't usually domain-specific. However, if you're applying for a very specific position and you have relevant knowledge that you usually don't include, it might be beneficial. For instance, I only include a course I completed in neurobiology when applying for relevant positions.

And at the end of the day, don't stress too much over your CV. I've heard stories of people who spent a lot of money to get professional help with their CVs, only to see no significant improvement in the response rate.

Now let's talk about how to define the job criteria you should be looking for.

Define What You Are Looking For

Before I start my job search, I find it helpful to come up with a list of "ideal" job criteria. This can quickly help me narrow down my options and guide my search. Here are the factors I usually consider:

1. The company's industry (like finance, healthcare, or real estate)

2. Minimum salary

3. Work format (remote, hybrid, or onsite)

4. Development field (back end, DevOps, machine learning)

5. Technologies used (Java, Kafka, Azure)

6. My role in the team (developer, lead)

7. Type of company (startup, product-based, consultancy, or outsourcing)

8. Benefits and perks (vacation days, insurance, shares)

9. Team size

10. Team structure

11. Company's main language for communication

12. Job security

For example, let's say I'm a Java developer with ten years of experience living in Oslo, Norway. I want to shift to functional languages, and I want to work in the well-being sector because I believe I can make a difference there. Also, since I'm an immigrant, using Norwegian at work would help me learn the language. Job security is not a big concern for me as I'm comfortable switching jobs. So, my criteria list might look like this:

1. **Industries**: Well-being, longevity, or education. Not interested in non-ESG companies

2. **Minimum Salary**: $100,000/year

3. **Work Format**: Onsite with a team in Oslo

4. **Development Field**: Back end, with some DevOps

5. **Technologies**: Scala

6. **Role**: Tech lead

7. **Type of Company**: Product-based

8. **Benefits**: Insurance, pension plan, shares

9. **Team Size**: Five to ten people

10. **Team Structure**: Dedicated product manager, UX, and QA

11. **Communication Language**: Norwegian

12. **Job Security**

The next useful step for me is to prioritize these criteria, so I know what's essential and what's not so important. For instance:

1. **Industries**: Well-being, longevity, or education. Not interested in non-ESG companies

2. **Technologies**: Scala

3. **Communication Language**: Norwegian

4. **Minimum Salary**: $100,000/year

5. **Development Field**: Back end, with some DevOps

6. **Work Format**: Onsite with a team in Oslo

7. **Role**: Tech lead

8. **Team Size**: Five to ten people

9. **Type of Company**: Product-based

10. **Team structure**: Dedicated product manager, UX, and QA

11. **Benefits**: Insurance, pension plan, shares

12. **Job Security**

Here, you can see that the most important part for me is the industry in which the company operates as it aligns with my values, and job security is the least important criterion for me in this job search.

Now, I have a priority list to guide my job search and filter out many irrelevant results. Some of these criteria can be applied right away in the search, like preferred technologies and roles. Others, like team structure and work format, will likely come up during the hiring process itself.

Search and Apply

Once I've used my priority list to filter options, there are usually still many open positions left. If not, it might be necessary to relax some of the less critical criteria. I aim to find around 10–20 positions that I could apply to. Some of these companies might seem like the perfect fit, while others could be considered backup options.

For the positions that really interest me, I usually write a cover letter. If there's a strong reason I want to work for them, it's beneficial to explain why. When I write this letter, I usually discuss why I like the position and what technical and nontechnical skills make me a good fit. To ensure I use good grammar and style, I often use ChatGPT. I provide it with the job description and a prompt like this: "Write a cover letter for this position. Make it brief and easy to read, and highlight that I'm a good fit because I like X about them and because I have skills Y and Z." If there's anything notable to mention, such as previous work with the company or past interviews, it's definitely worth including.

Next, let's talk about how to do some background checks on a company.

The Reference Check Is for Your Benefit

Candidates are often asked to share references so that potential employers can understand their work history and behavior at previous workplaces. I find it helpful to flip this around and check out the company you might join as well.

One effective way to learn about a new company is to directly ask its employees or your potential future team members. If possible, find people you might work with and others in the company in general, and ask them what they like and don't like about the company. You might also find someone a few people who have worked at the company before, and they could give you even more honest insights because they're not currently tied to the company. I typically get tremendously useful insights from former employees. What I typically try to accomplish is to find red flags about the company.

Typically, I ask the following questions:

- Why did you decide to leave the company? (if it is a former employee)

- What do you enjoy most about working at this company, and what do you like least?

- Has the company supported your professional growth, and if so, how?

- Are there any coworkers you particularly enjoy or don't enjoy working with?

- How many people have left the company in the past year? (A high turnover rate can be a red flag.)

- Do you have any financial investment in the company? (If they could invest but haven't, they may not have faith in the company's future. But be aware that in some cases, as with waiting to exercise your options, it is not a red flag as it can be simply economically beneficial to postpone it.)

- How often have you had to work overtime?

- How has your salary grown during your time at the company? (Significant growth can indicate that the company values its employees and understands the cost of hiring new ones.)

These questions will provide a good overview of the companies as they are mostly about what has already happened, so it is harder to add fluffy answers.

Also, there are websites like Glassdoor where you can find company reviews, salary estimates, and other insights. Make sure to look at this or a similar one before you apply; it can give you a clearer picture of what the company is like.

Now that you've applied to a bunch of positions, the first stages of the hiring process begin: finding out more details about the position and initial screening calls. These steps can take a lot of time and can feel repetitive, so let's talk about how to handle them effectively.

How to Be Likable

Being friendly helps a lot when you're trying to get a job. I've seen smart people not get jobs because they didn't show their best side. It's not about lying or bragging. It's about showing what you're good at when it matters. Here are some tips.

Be nice and respectful. No one likes rude or full-of-themselves people. Treat people's time as valuable as your own. The way you talk to people on the interview shows what working with you might be like, so try to leave a good impression. It's also good if ask the interviewer questions that help you both connect. For example, asking "What made you smile today?" can be a good start.

Also, know who you're talking to. For example, you'll need to talk about your technical skills in different ways depending on who you're talking to: a recruiter, a manager, or the tech team. In general, the recruiter is looking for your people skills, the tech team wants to see your technical knowledge, and the manager wants to see both and how you can contribute to the company's success. Make sure you talk about the right parts of your experience when you're talking to them.

If you're feeling sick or too tired to give a good impression, you might want to think about rescheduling the interview. I've seen people come sick to their second interviews and got refused in the end because they weren't as engaged as in their first one.

Showing that you love what you do can also make you stand out. Even if it is something nerdy, being excited about what you do can get everyone's attention. Talk about what you love and why. If it's relevant, share what you geek out about. Showing a bit of your true self can be genuine and appealing.

With this knowledge, let's proceed to our first interaction with the recruiter.

Asynchronous Communication

When you're contacted by a hiring person and they offer a call to discuss details, I find it more efficient to chat or email for the information I need. You want to know whether it's worth investing time in the hiring process. If you set salary as your main requirement and it is not stated on the vacancy, why would you go on a call and spend one hour of your and the company's time just to figure out that the salary is simply below your minimum requirement?

Typically, the vacancy will lack some information about the list of criteria you set, so it's important to clarify all of the missing bits, for example, whether the team is collocated and what the company's daily language is.

After you get this info, you might be asked for a prescreening call. This is another point that almost always gives me a feeling, "this could have been an email" kind of feeling, as they're usually alike each time. They'll tell you about the company, the project, and the hiring process and ask about your experience, what you're looking for, and when you can start. This could easily be covered in an email, so why do we need a call?

The reason isn't about information but because the company wants to get a feel for you as a person. One solution I've found is to ask for a list of questions and then send back a video of my answers. This is easier to schedule and generally takes less time.

Also, some companies like to give "The Big Five Personality Test" at this step, so you can do it once and reuse it as well.

However, if you are asked to have a call, it is important to use it to your benefit. Beyond the formal checks and explaining common things about the company, the prescreening can turn into a proper interview process step that provides both you and the employer deeper insights into how you both behave and respond if you ask good questions.

Here are some questions you might want to ask either during a prescreening call or at a later stage:

- Why is this position open?

- What's your onboarding process?

- What are the company's values?

- Who are your customers?

- What HR processes do you have in place?

- What benefits do you offer?

- Do you have performance reviews?

- How often do you review salaries?

With these steps, you can luckily get quickly through the introduction stage and then move on to the technical round.

Technical Round

Remember that the technical interview isn't just for the company to judge you but also for you to figure out if you like the team as these are directly the people you are going to work with. Don't be afraid to ask questions that will help you understand the team, their processes, and their technical expertise. Here are some questions I usually ask:

- How would you describe an ideal candidate for this role?

- Who are the other developers on the team, and what are their areas of expertise?

- What kind of processes does the team follow?

- How involved are the tech team in making product decisions?

- How is your deployment set up?

- Can you describe the architecture of the project?

- What's your approach to testing, code review, and refactoring?

- Do you have any external integrations?

- What technical challenges are you currently facing?

- What are the technical plans for the project in the next few months?

- What are the tasks you are working on right now?

These questions should give you a good understanding of the project, and you will be better prepared for the round with the manager.

Manager Round

Managers are essential to provide a bigger overview of the company, so sometimes it is only they who can answer questions like these:

- How would you describe an ideal candidate for this role?

- Where does the company's money come from?

- What is the company planning to do in the next one and three years?

- What are the biggest problems in the company right now?

- How will the company measure my job performance?

- What do you want me to achieve in the first 30, 60, and 90 days of work?

- Do you give special rewards to employees who do an outstanding job?

- Could you share an example of a recent project or initiative that didn't go as planned recently?

- What other activities can a developer be involved in besides project work?

- How does the company help employees learn and grow?

- Does the company have a culture of mentoring?

- What could my career path in this company look like?

- What's the company's policy on working overtime?

- Will I have regular one-on-one meetings with you?

Test assignments typically come before or after the manager round. Let's discuss how we can handle it in the most efficient manner.

Test Assignment

At a certain stage, it's usual to provide some kind of evidence that you can write quality code. Often, this comes in the form of a take-home test assignment. If I'm asked to do such an assignment, I typically respond with several alternatives, ordered by my preference:

1. I can show pull requests (PRs) I've made.

2. I can demonstrate some of the projects I've created.

3. I can present previous test assignments I've completed.

4. I can do the test assignment if it's paid.

Let's break down this list. The length of assignment tasks can greatly vary, and sometimes companies might give you a test task that could take up to ten hours, expecting you to do it without compensation. I find this approach disrespectful.

Firstly, typical test tasks reveal very little about a person's real-life coding ability. PRs, for instance, are usually more revealing. Secondly, a developer's time is valuable, so it's strange to expect a lengthy task to be completed for free. As a result, I prefer to offer a few alternatives that are less time-consuming for me and provide a better demonstration of my expertise to the tech interviewer.

How to Negotiate a Salary

When it comes to salary, there are a few handy tips to keep in mind.

First off, you need to know what's a fair salary range for your job role in the field and ideally inside the company as well. Do some research on what developers with similar experience to yours are making in the same area and in the company. This way, you won't set your sights too high or too low.

Remember, when you quote your lower salary range, that's often what you'll be offered, or maybe even a bit less; it's rarely more. So, it's a good plan to set your lower limit at the actual amount you'd be happy to accept.

If you've got other job options on the table, they can be a big help when negotiating salary. Don't be shy about saying that you've got other interviews or even other offers. This could give you a leg up in negotiating a better deal. And even if you don't have another offer, usually a company can bump up their offer a little when they send it to you. This extra bit, often called a "counteroffer budget," typically ranges from 5% to 20%. More than 50% of employers are fine to negotiate the salary [2], so it's usually okay to say that you were hoping for a slightly higher number and that you'd sign the contract right away if they could add, say, 5–10%.

How to Get an Even Deeper Understanding of a Team

Okay, so the job meets your criteria well, and you're enthusiastic about the technical aspects of the project. But as we all know, many things can seem bright and exciting at the start. However, once you begin working, you might encounter small details that you didn't consider before. Maybe, after a week, you notice that the developers are unmotivated and unfriendly or there's a rigid hierarchy where your ideas and initiatives aren't considered.

You might start to wish, "If only I could've known what the job would feel like before I accepted the offer." The good news is, there's a method that allows for such an experience.

Once, during my interview process with Volkswagen, I was told that the final step would be spending a day working with the team. I would meet the team members, work on an assigned task, participate in their meetings, observe the office environment, sense the team's dynamics, and get a feel for the company culture. Although I ultimately chose not to proceed with them, this process seemed greatly beneficial for both parties. It can provide insights into the inner workings of a company and help determine early on if it's a good fit. Despite the effort required to organize this, it offers immense value, and I would certainly request such an opportunity the next time I receive a job offer. It allows you to understand your future workplace earlier and make a more informed decision.

If such a process doesn't exist, you can still ask to spend some time with the team before signing the contract. Perhaps you could do some pair programming for a couple of hours, attend a few meetings, or join their after-work gathering. Any of these activities could provide valuable insights that might be hard to acquire otherwise.

Read Your Contract Well

Some contracts might be trickier than others. Personally, I typically feel worse after reading one. This is because all of its benefits have been already mentioned to me many times, and now I have to go through all the limiting and less pleasant parts of the contract. For example, I've seen contracts that don't allow you to take part in any organized activity without your CEO's approval and that you have to dedicate all your manpower to the company. If this sounds a little bit too much, you're right, but such things do exist, and they are popular. So, it's vital to read the contract carefully and get legal help if needed.

If there's anything in the contract you don't get, ask them to clarify it formally. An email works fine. This way, you have their explanation on record, and you can refer to it if there's a disagreement later on. And if there's something in the contract you're not okay with, make sure to ask them to change it. The company might say they never enforce certain things, but if it's in your contract, that's what you'll be judged by later on. So, don't assume that everyone will play nice if things go wrong and you need to discuss something legally.

Use the Test Period

Congrats, you've done well, and now you have a job offer. One thing I'd highlight is to agree on a fair trial period where you and the company can decide to part ways quickly if things aren't working out if this is not already included in your contract. This gives you a good chance to stop and move on after a few weeks if you realize the workplace isn't right for you.

Summary

I think finding a great job is much easier if you know what you're looking for and try to learn as much as possible about the company, the project, the processes, and the team during the interview. So don't hesitate to ask the interviewer lots of questions because an interview is a two-way process.

- **Understand Market Conditions**: Be more agreeable in challenging times like during massive layoffs.

- **Preparation Phase**:

  - **Avoid Rushing**: Begin job searches when not pressured.

- **Target Companies**: List five to ten favored companies and monitor their openings.

- **Utilize Job Search Websites**: Save searches to get constant updates.

- **Stay Interview-Ready**: Occasionally attend interviews to stay sharp.

- **Personal References and Networking**:

  - 70–85% of jobs aren't advertised. Personal references enhance chances.

  - Connect with target company employees through events, conferences, or direct outreach.

- **Effective CV**:

  - **Update Regularly**: Refresh CV periodically to capture all achievements.

  - *Structure*: Important details first. Aim for quick readability.

  - **Feedback**: Seek opinions from varied professionals: recruiter, manager, technical person.

- **Defining Job Criteria**:

  - **List and Prioritize Desired Job Aspects**: Industry, salary, work format, technologies, role, company type, benefits, and others.

- **Job Application Process**:

  - **Filter**: Use a priority list to identify suitable positions.

  - **Apply**: Around 10–20 positions. Craft personalized cover letters for top picks. Use tools like ChatGPT for assistance.

113

- **Background Checks on Companies**:
  - **Directly Ask Employees**: Learn about company culture, professional growth, turnover rate, and more.
  - **Utilize Review Platforms**: Websites like Glassdoor offer company insights.

- **Be Likable**:
  - Respect everyone's time.
  - Adjust communication based on audience (recruiter, manager, tech team).
  - Show passion for your work.

- **Initial Communication**: Prefer asynchronous communication for initial discussions.

- **Prescreening**:
  - Consider sending video responses to questions.
  - Ask HR-related questions.

- **Technical Round**:
  - Understand the team, their challenges, and work culture.
  - Evaluate the team's technical knowledge.

- **Manager Round**: Understand company vision, challenges, and expectations.

- **Test Assignment**: Offer alternatives like past PRs or paid assignments.

- **Salary Negotiation**:

  - Research average salaries for your role.

  - Have other offers on the table.

  - Consider counteroffering.

- **Understanding the Team**: Spend a day with the potential team to assess fit.

- **Contract Review**:

  - Read thoroughly; seek clarifications.

  - Get any verbal promises in writing.

- **Test Period**: Use it to identify if you indeed like the company.

References

[1]   www.payscale.com/career-advice/many-jobs-found-networking/

[2]   https://press.careerbuilder.com/2017-10-27-More-Than-Half-of-Workers-Do-Not-Negotiate-Job-Offers-According-to-New-CareerBuilder-Survey

PART II

Mindset

In the rapidly evolving world of software engineering, the ability to code is just one piece of the puzzle. A healthy, productive mindset is equally crucial, one that not only propels you forward but also equips you to navigate the highs and lows of the journey. This part is intended to shed light on the crucial elements of such a mindset:

Chapter 9, "Lifelong Learning," establishes the claim that in the face of constant change, continuous learning is not a good-to-have, but a necessity. We dive into the importance of curiosity, stepping out of comfort zones, and the inevitability of learning at all stages of one's career. This section underscores how equipping oneself with knowledge and skills can build resilience against the fear of job loss or instability.

Chapter 10, "Collaboration," explores the value of fostering long-lasting, productive relationships in the workplace. Building on the notion of compound interest, we discuss how consistent efforts in empathy, communication, and networking can yield significant returns over time. This section also delves into practical advice on dealing with challenging interpersonal dynamics and ensuring your work is recognized and appreciated.

Chapter 11, "Values," will guide you through the process of identifying your core values and why they matter when choosing a job. This is a crucial step often overlooked during job hunting, leading to dissatisfaction and disengagement despite having the right skills for the job.

Chapter 12, "Health," underscores the importance of holistic well-being in sustaining productivity and motivation. Here, we provide practical advice on maintaining physical health through sleep, nutrition, and exercise, as well as tips for nurturing mental well-being.

Chapter 13, "Company Attitude," takes a look at how a positive mindset toward your employer and manager can transform your workplace experience. We'll discuss strategies to cultivate a win-win mentality, dismantle the negative aspects of "us vs. them" thinking, and work toward mutual goals.

Chapter 14, "Handling Failures," approaches failure as an essential component of the learning process. Here, you'll learn to embrace your mistakes and those of others as invaluable learning opportunities.

CHAPTER 9

Lifelong Learning

There are two key reasons to learn: to become a software engineer and to remain a software engineer. The first reason is clear, but the second is a bit more interesting. Software engineering is a field where new information, tools, methods, and languages are constantly emerging. As I write this, new personal coding assistants based on large text models appear all the time, and I believe they'll significantly change how I code a year from now. So, you can either fall behind, stagnate, and gradually become outdated, or you can keep up with changes. Embracing change is vital; without it, it's tough to stay up-to-date.

When I started development in 2017, jQuery was a pretty hot technology. It had some competitors, but it was strong and dominant. Back then, a front-end developer with primary knowledge of jQuery was a wanted person. In 2023, it is almost impossible to find jQuery as a required skill in vacancies. While a lot of existing websites are still built with its help (meaning, they need support), I would be surprised to hear a story that somebody managed to find a new well-paid job while knowing only jQuery.

And there are plenty of such examples of rises and falls just in the last five years—MySQL, Backbone, DigitalOcean, Vagrant, Apache HTTP Server, Bootstrap—once very hot and new technologies, but now, if not gone, then at least, almost never met on new projects. The field is changing all the time, new, better, or quicker players replace the well-established technologies. And the technologies and tools we focus on now are barely excluded from the tendency.

© Mykyta Chernenko 2023
M. Chernenko, *The Rational Software Engineer*,
https://doi.org/10.1007/978-1-4842-9795-7_9

This is why I consider the mindset of lifelong learning to be essential for a software engineer.

Curiosity

Being curious is a key reason why many software engineers choose and enjoy this field. It's common for us to ask a lot of "whys" and question the way things are. This journey involves admitting many mistakes and gaining insights, which is actually very hurtful for the ego—the things that make me love the process even more.

Many practices and processes have assumptions and rules we often take for granted. I've seen people react negatively just to hearing the word "waterfall" or finding out a team doesn't fully use Agile. But every team I've worked with combines techniques from different approaches, including waterfall. I realized after some time and curiosity that there's no such thing as a "bad" methodology, they're tools just like programming languages. Saying waterfall is a terrible methodology is like saying C is a bad language. Tools are good when used in the right situations. And to understand technology or methodology deeply and when it is appropriate, we need to be curious about it in the first place.

To be curious means to ask a lot of "why," and there are many ways to do it. For instance, one principle in my team is "no questions are stupid." I think this is a good rule for creating a supportive, knowledge-sharing, trust-building environment. Ask your colleagues why they chose a certain technology or approach, ask your tech lead about your processes, ask your manager about the company strategy, and ask your product manager about your feature road map. Trying to challenge assumptions and being curious about principles and internals is a true game changer when it comes to understanding the field we operate in. This is often a difference between an engineer who progresses and learns quickly and one who stagnates—the former is curious about why the thing works in a certain way.

Now, let's talk about whether everyone needs to learn.

Seniors Don't Need to Learn

Some folks believe that as you gain experience, you don't need to learn as much or be as curious as before. I disagree. When I started, my knowledge was limited. I only needed to know enough to complete my work. I just had to understand the web framework I was using, how to use a few libraries, and follow the security advice for the framework even though I didn't fully understand what CSRF and XSS attacks were.

Back then, trying to understand everything deeply would have been too much. So, it made sense to figure out the bare minimum and learn "just enough" to finish the job. But as I learned more, and my knowledge base expanded, I started asking "why" more, not less. Almost every day, I find something interesting that I want to explore further, so I make a note to read more about it later. Often, I don't have time to read everything I want to even though I wish I could. And I still have "aha" moments fairly often when I learn something new or realize I was wrong about something.

And to stop or slow down on this journey and consider that you have learned enough is simply to be cocky. The learning never stops, and the ones who think they've had enough become worse of the engineers over time. So stay clear of this thought—we will never know enough to stop learning.

Let's cover a little bit more how constant learning relates to the comfort zone.

Comfort Zone

Learning something new often means stepping just beyond your comfort zone. This is a skill that I find crucial for improving as a software engineer. When I'm learning something and it doesn't feel challenging, it's a sign that I can push myself more. Pushing myself helps in two ways. Firstly, it speeds up my learning and helps me understand things more deeply. Secondly, taking on more challenging tasks is simply fun.

When I feel at ease learning my first programming language, I want to start learning a different one. After I get a good grasp of object-oriented programming patterns, I find it enjoyable to try functional programming paradigms. When I can find information quickly from text sources, I try learning from video guides. And once I understand I can easily find answers to a problem with a library on the coding forums, I start digging into the source code to find answers. All of that should be used to be constantly accustomed to stepping out of our comfort zone as this is just another important skill that we need to learn and then keep up.

The software industry rewards problem-solvers and innovators—individuals who aren't afraid to tackle the unknown. So, stepping out of your comfort zone not only increases your knowledge and skills but also helps to demonstrate your value as a proactive and adaptable engineer.

Next, let's see how learning is crucial for your career in general.

Learning and Employment

Constant learning and growing can help you in your employment in many ways. First, by learning new things and staying up-to-date, you make sure you're always valuable to employers. If you understand that your current job doesn't provide you with all the necessary knowledge that you need to be greatly attractive for future hiring, it's a good idea to pay attention to what skills are in demand and incorporate them into your learning plan. This gives you a lot of confidence because you know that if you're not happy at your current job, it won't be too scary to leave and find a new one.

By keeping your skills up-to-date, you're less scared of getting fired. You also feel more confident standing up for your values, speaking out when needed, and not putting up with unfairness. Losing a job is never easy, but it's much harder if your skills are outdated or not useful anymore.

Also, try to work on projects at your job that use technologies that are popular in the market. You don't want to become the person who knows a lot about a technology that's only used at your company. This can become a bigger problem if your company mostly uses its own in-house solutions rather than widely used technologies and languages. This kind of specialized knowledge often isn't useful to other companies, so try to avoid it.

The last pitfall to avoid in the job market is becoming too invested in a single popular technology. This could happen for several reasons. You might think a certain technology, like Ruby on Rails, is a safe bet because it's been around for a while. Alternatively, you may be attracted to a new, superior technology believing it's the future of job opportunities. Unfortunately, these trends are often unpredictable.

In the past, Angular, React, and Vue were engaged in a fierce competition. Among them, Vue seemed to me the most elegant, clear, and user-friendly choice. I had hoped this would help it dominate the market, but surprisingly, React emerged as the winner. This was despite React being the least appealing to me from most viewpoints. Similarly, when Rust began gaining traction, I believed it would overtake the C, C++ space rather quickly, but that didn't happen. And despite Java's wide usage, it was eventually outperformed by Python and even more so by JavaScript in back-end development.

The bottom line is to not stake your career on a single technology. Instead, keep a constant eye on current trends and adapt accordingly. This approach is far more important for maintaining job market relevance.

Summary

- Embrace lifelong learning to keep up with constantly emerging tools, methods, and languages in software engineering.

- Cultivate curiosity; ask "why" about technologies, methodologies, and practices. Don't be afraid to admit mistakes.

- Seniors also need to learn; experience should increase curiosity and deepen understanding.

- Regularly step outside your comfort zone to accelerate learning and improve problem-solving skills.

- Actively learn about and work with trending technologies to remain valuable to employers.

- Avoid becoming overly specialized in a technology used solely at your company or simply the one you like the most. Aim for a balance between specialized and general knowledge.

CHAPTER 10

Collaboration

In most workplaces, we seldom work alone. We interact with teammates, collaborate with other teams, report to managers, and communicate with clients, among others. Such interactions constitute a significant part of our working hours. Therefore, it is crucial to establish nourishing, mutually beneficial relationships with our coworkers. Not only does this contribute to a more pleasant work environment, but it also aids in our professional growth. As Naval Ravikant once said, "Play long-term games with long-term people... All returns in life, whether in wealth, relationships, or knowledge, come from compound interest" [1]. If we aim to play the long-term game, we must base our progress on solid relationships with the people we work with. So, how do we build good relationships with our colleagues?

Becoming a Pleasant Colleague

Maintaining good relationships with colleagues not only contributes to a satisfactory work environment [2] but also boosts your performance [3]. Therefore, it's essential to consciously strive for effective collaboration. Here's a list of actionable points I follow to become a better coworker:

- Don't assume you're smarter than others. Firstly, it's likely untrue. Secondly, it's an attitude that benefits no one. Everyone has strengths and weaknesses. Treating others as if they're unintelligent only damages relationships.

M. Chernenko, *The Rational Software Engineer*,
https://doi.org/10.1007/978-1-4842-9795-7_10

- Help others grow and learn if they are open to it. Provide constructive feedback when people are willing to accept it and share useful knowledge or materials.

- Assist others when they're stuck. Be open to participating in architecture reviews for other teams or sharing your experience with a particular tool with a new team that wants to implement it in their pipeline. Be approachable and helpful.

- Manage your negative emotions effectively. The workplace is not a place for outbursts or confrontations. If you've acted inappropriately, apologize.

- Make commitments you can keep so others can trust your word and plan accordingly.

- Accept that others, like yourself, are allowed to make mistakes as it is a part of learning.

- Don't complain without solving. You may want to vent to your colleagues, but to them, it will feel like a problem they need to solve themselves, especially if you do it repeatedly and don't take actions to ease the issue.

Effective communication with teammates is especially crucial during emotional moments or conflicts. The outcome of such situations can vary greatly depending on whether you communicate effectively or poorly. In his book, *Therapist's Toolkit*, David D. Burns, MD, provides five principles to enhance communication during these times:

- **Validation**: Always try to identify and acknowledge an element of truth in what the other person is saying, even if it might seem unfair or unreasonable to you.

- **Empathy**: Make an effort to place yourself in the other person's shoes and genuinely attempt to "see the world through their eyes." This involves both acknowledging their feelings and summarizing their words to ensure they feel heard.

- **Inquiry**: When needed, ask gentle, probing questions to delve deeper into the issue and truly understand the other person's perspective.

- **I Statement**: If you need to convey your feelings or stance on the situation, frame your sentiments using "I" statements. For instance, in a situation when a manager comes to you and pushes an additional deadline, which will clearly make you feel overwhelmed, instead of saying "I won't do this for you!" you can express it as "I feel emotionally pressured with this additional deadline."

- **Stroking**: Regardless of the disagreement's intensity, always try to offer a genuine positive remark or compliment about the other person. This gesture communicates respect, showing that even in disagreements, you still value and appreciate them."

Remember that every interaction you have in the workplace forms an impression about you. Your technical skills, your ability to collaborate, your demeanor, and your problem-solving capabilities all contribute to this impression. These factors will significantly influence your future professional relationships, such as how willing others might be to assist you, collaborate on a project with you, provide a reference, or avoid you.

Keeping these points in mind will likely make you a pleasant person to work with, benefiting both you and your colleagues. While it's enjoyable and rewarding to work with good people, having a strategy to deal with challenging relationships is also necessary.

How to Deal with Unpleasant People

In the realm of software engineering, I firmly believe there's no place for jerks. Generally, I've found the majority of individuals are great to interact with. Every now and then, someone may behave poorly, but usually, they realize their mistake and apologize. However, it's a different story when a person consistently behaves negatively.

If a generally good person falls short of expectations—perhaps they're regularly late to stand-ups, or they habitually rewrite other people's code at night—it's important to address the issue. Giving them constructive feedback, either directly or through their manager, can be helpful. More often than not, people have the capacity to change and improve.

But when you are dealing with somebody who behaves in a way that constantly spoils the day for other coworkers, the best course of action is to get rid of such people as soon as possible. I don't tolerate such behavior in the workplace, and I hope you won't either. Our collective goal should be to reduce such behavior within our industry and to foster a more positive environment at our companies. To illustrate this, let me share an experience.

Once I had to deal with a pretty toxic ML engineer on my team. His behavior included losing his temper over constructive code review comments, blaming everyone but himself for missed deadlines, and even shouting at the CEO and other colleagues during meetings. He would send offensive messages on Slack, delete them, and then deny writing them. This behavior forced us to establish a rule of only communicating with him through public channels. Furthermore, his technical abilities didn't compensate for his behavior—his code quality was poor, and he struggled to integrate his ML model into the production code. The startup company kept him on board because they lacked the budget for a better replacement.

Though I didn't work directly with him often, his treatment of my colleagues was infuriating. Backed by another consultant who had a more managerial position and was also frustrated with his behavior, we decided to take a stand. We presented management with two options: either our entire consulting team would leave, or the ML engineer would be dismissed. Although we were unlikely to leave and it was mostly a bluff, our message was clear, and the management issued a final warning to him. His behavior improved for a month, so it finally became bearable to with him, and after that, he chose to leave. He then joined a FAANG company, and I truly hope he's changed his behavior for his team's sake.

Poor treatment of others inevitably leads to a poor impression. Such people may wonder why others are unwilling to assist them, avoid their requests, and treat them badly in general, but often it is because they're themselves unpleasant to interact with.

Let's move on to the topic of expanding your professional network and why it's crucial.

Effective Networking

Having a good network can be helpful in many different ways. It can offer help when you are stuck, let you make new friends, bring job opportunities, and give you a chance to join fun events such as conferences and trips. But sometimes, making more connections can feel like a hard task that does not give you anything right away. I know a lot of people who find it difficult to meet others and make new friends, either in person or online.

Even though meeting new people can be tough for me too, I often find that it ends up being a great thing. I want to share two of my own experiences that started from small beginnings and became something much bigger.

One time, I saw an advertisement for a channel on Telegram that was about books, thoughts, and startup ideas. It was not a very big group, but I found it interesting and decided to join. A couple of days later, the person who made the channel wrote a post about himself. At the end of the post, he wrote, "I am also looking for a technical cofounder to join me." This came as a surprise, and I wasn't sure what to do. I found it intriguing and a bit scary, but I decided to give it a try. I thought that in the worst-case scenario, I would have a chat with a smart person, and then we would decide to go our separate ways. But things did not turn out that way. We liked each other's ideas and decided to try to work together to create a startup. This led us to try out many different ideas over a year, and finally, we came up with one that seemed promising: an app called Nemlys that helps couples communicate better through personalized AI questions and reflections. Now, we have a team of three people, and we have our first 1,000 users.

Another important introduction happened outside of the work networking context, the story of how I met my wife. I felt that I was ready to find a serious relationship and tried out different popular ways to meet new people. This led to two years of going on many dates and lots of funny stories. Even though the process involved a lot of different partners, it all was in vain. I couldn't really find somebody I saw the future with. But then, I met Yuliia by chance when she was working at a food court. After I made an order, I decided to talk to her because I thought she might also be from Ukraine, and I was right. Even though asking someone out at a food court might not seem like the most effective way to find a life partner and I totally wouldn't believe that this is how I really found one despite all of the other efforts I put in, that is what happened to me.

Of course, there have been many times when meeting new people with good potential did not lead to anything big. But you never know what could happen when you take a chance and talk to a new person, whether it's at work or somewhere else. That's why I always try to make my social circle bigger. Even though I'm not very good at it, it has already brought many good things into my life.

It's also important to build strong relationships, not just make more acquaintances. One good friend can be more valuable than 100 people you just know casually. And having 100 people who think well of you is better than 1000 people who have no opinion or a bad opinion of you.

So, how can you build a good network?

- Focus on the right people. Think about who could be most helpful for your career or your projects, and be ready to meet them wherever you go.

- Try to create win-win situations. Don't just take from people or expect them to do things for you. Instead, be the first to offer help, and create mutually beneficial situations.

- Connect people who should meet each other. Others will see this and might do the same for you.

- Remember that you can also network online. I have people in my network whom I have never met in person, but I know I can give them a strong recommendation.

- Make good impressions.

- Join communities and contribute. This could be working on an open source project or helping to organize a conference.

- Meet people in settings where you share a common interest. It's easier to connect with people at events like hackathons, conferences, school, or at work because you are already in the same place.

So we have covered how to talk to your colleagues and expand your networking, and what about your manager?

Manager Is Your Friend

Our manager should be like a friend. They ought to understand your goals, values, and personal challenges. If my company has a system that allows regular communication and feedback with the management, that's excellent. However, if such a system isn't in place, I'm not hesitant to approach the management myself and schedule regular meetings with them.

The Essentials of 1:1 Meetings

Whether formal or more casual, it's crucial to hold meetings with your manager. These meetings serve as a platform to improve, address, and share numerous things. Here are a few points I usually concentrate on during my 1:1s:

- Ensure it doesn't turn into a stand-up. This is not about reporting what you've completed or planned for your project.

- Make it clear that you desire recognition for your efforts if it's lacking. Feeling appreciated at work significantly impacts job satisfaction. It's beneficial to discuss whether you prefer public or private praise. While you may feel vulnerable mentioning this, it's usually sufficient to express your need for constructive feedback from management, helping you perform well enough to receive explicit appreciation.

- Talk about the most effective way to provide feedback on your work, how often you should receive feedback, and from whom. If you make mistakes or perform poorly, how should this be addressed? Make an effort to describe what form of feedback works best for you.

- Discuss your career path and future growth. Your manager plays a crucial role in ensuring you are satisfied with your professional development. They can assist you in finding learning opportunities that match your interests.

- Discuss the different methods to facilitate your learning. Whether you want to secure mentorship or require specific resources or courses, they may be able to recommend something. You can also inquire about their opinion on the most effective way to progress in your desired direction.

- Get clear on their expectations for your current role and future prospects. Understanding this will help guide your efforts. You might assume that the manager expects you to produce as much code as possible, but in reality, they might be more interested in you facilitating better interteam collaboration.

- Discuss your current work pace and whether it's sustainable. Is your work-life balance in check?

- Share any ideas or initiatives you'd like to implement to improve the company.

Fixing Issues

Management should be the first point of contact for nontechnical problems that crop up during your work. By "management," I don't just mean your direct manager. It could be anyone who can help you solve your problem: team lead, CTO, HR, and so on.

When an issue arises that requires their input, I typically write to them outlining the problem and requesting a suitable time for discussion. Sometimes, they might resolve it via chat, or they may prefer to have a face-to-face meeting. Quite often, managers can work wonders in resolving issues.

When Your Manager Says No

Occasionally, you might find that management is unable or unwilling to help you solve an issue. As discouraging as this may feel, there are a few points to consider:

- Did you communicate your problem clearly? With critical issues causing frustration, it's important to be assertive. Sometimes, a manager might think you are okay, but not entirely satisfied, while in reality, you may be experiencing considerable distress. If a critical issue arises, ensure you've communicated it clearly.

- Managers usually have more context than you do. This is something I try to remember when things don't go as planned. There might be events within the company that you're unaware of that influence their decisions. The manager who didn't want to give me VPN access could be ordered to minimize access. The manager who asked me to work overtime may have been dealing with serious company budget constraints.

- Ultimately, it's my decision on what I can and cannot tolerate. I might be okay doing CSS work because the project can't afford a dedicated professional for a month, but I wouldn't accept doing it 70% of the time for a year.

Summary

- Foster positive relationships in the workplace by valuing individual strengths, providing constructive feedback, helping others, and managing your emotions professionally.

- Deal with unpleasant colleagues by addressing issues directly or through management; advocate for a healthy work environment by refusing to tolerate consistently negative individuals.

- Expand your professional network by focusing on quality relationships, creating win-win situations, and joining communities or events where shared interests can build connections.

- Approach management openly and regularly, discussing topics such as recognition, feedback, career path, and work pace, to ensure mutual understanding and job satisfaction. Consider the broader context behind their decisions, and ultimately, make decisions about what you can tolerate in the workplace.

References

[1]   Play Long-term Games With Long-term People, https://nav.al/long-term

[2]   LinkedIn Study Reveals Work BFFs Make Us Happier at the Office, https://blog.linkedin.com/2014/07/08/work-bffs

[3]   Are Workplace Friendships a Mixed Blessing?
      Exploring Tradeoffs of Multiplex Relationships
      and their Associations with Job Performance,
      `https://onlinelibrary.wiley.com/doi/`
      `abs/10.1111/peps.12109`

CHAPTER 11

Values

Writing code can feel like a game. When writing a challenging piece of code, you might find that time flies without you even realizing it. Some coding puzzles can captivate you to the point where you're up late tackling that "one last thing" or find yourself pondering over it during your leisure hours. But what makes it even more fulfilling is writing code for a project that corresponds to your values. It is what differentiates a game for the sake of the game itself and a game with ultimate meaning. And it is also beneficial both for your job satisfaction and productivity [1] because, well, if you care for what you do, you typically enjoy doing it and do it better.

At my first job, I was creating websites for businesses in Belgium. It was interesting as everything was fresh to me. However, I can't say making a management system for aquaparks was particularly rewarding. I vividly recall the day when I was assigned to work on a project to develop exercises for children with dyslexia. As someone who enjoys teaching, gaming, and helping others, I was so thrilled with the idea that it kept me awake, thinking of all the exciting features I could build. That level of enthusiasm was new to me, and it made me realize that values actually matter a lot, it is not only the technology that makes my work meaningful.

Unfortunately, I also see many people exploring career opportunities without thoroughly considering their values. It's common for a candidate to focus on the tech stack of a company in an interview, and there are numerous job search platforms that let you find roles based on specific technical skills. While technology is crucial, it's just one part of the story. I'd rather have job search platforms that list all software engineering roles

© Mykyta Chernenko 2023
M. Chernenko, *The Rational Software Engineer*,
https://doi.org/10.1007/978-1-4842-9795-7_11

in specific fields like child care, volunteer organizations, or those fighting fake news so that I can find positions aligned with my values. And, surely, it's also important to understand what a company does and its mission, not just its tech stack during an interview.

Values clearly matter, but most engineers don't have them aligned and matched at their jobs. So what are the most common reasons why people don't have a job according to their values? I see the following ones:

- Lack of values awareness

- Focus on practical considerations

- Limited options

- Pressure from others

- Lack of clear results from their efforts

Let's discuss them a little bit closer.

Lack of Values Awareness

Surely, you can't find a company that matches your values unless you understand what matters to you first. To kick-start this self-reflection, here are some questions you might find helpful:

- What problems in the world or my surroundings do I deeply care about?

- How can I make a difference in the world and shape it into a place where I'd love to be?

- Which hobbies or topics hold my interest the most?

- Which company would make me proud to be a part of?

When I was brainstorming ideas for my startup, identifying my values was crucial because working on something meaningful makes a significant difference. To give you an idea of what a values list might look like, here's what I came up with:

- Spreading truthful information amid a sea of misinformation

  - Supporting scientific endeavors

  - Fighting against fake news

- Creating emotional experiences for people

  - Enhancing the quality of social interactions and relationships

  - Promoting enjoyable experiences, rest, and events

  - Solving social issues and assisting people in various forms of distress

  - Addressing the adverse effects of COVID-19 on individuals

- Personal development and self-improvement

  - Promoting well-being in areas such as health, fitness, nutrition, sleep, and mental wellness

  - Improving productivity

  - Engaging in projects related to brain function and improvement

  - Helping transhumanism—using technology to enhance our physical selves

- Using AI to improve people's lives and automate mundane tasks

- Encouraging efficient learning

Creating a list like this can help identify the key areas that you care about. Once you've done that, you can begin to see how these might fit within the field of software engineering.

For instance, if you feel strongly about environmental preservation, you could look for companies that are working on cleaning up forests or lakes and check if they need help building their technologies. It's also common to search among startups as they often involve some sort of new software development. While it can be a bit more challenging to translate the values into the exact criteria for your job search, at least you'll have a clearer idea of whether a job opportunity sent by a recruiter aligns with your values.

Focus on Practical Considerations

When hunting for a job, many people tend to focus on factors like the technology stack, salary, benefits, or the job's location. These factors are undoubtedly important, and prioritizing values might require making some compromises, especially in terms of your salary. But it is also important to remember how much it pays off. It creates a difference between a job with and without meaning, and there are a lot of young people who understand it. In this study [2], 40% of young workers state that a company's mission is their most crucial job criterion.

From my perspective, I'd rather work in a place where the pay is just sufficient but the company's mission resonates with my own values than in a place that offers a 50% higher salary but lacks meaning for me or, worse, operates contrary to my values.

Limited Options

Getting a job that lines up with your values can be tough, especially when many businesses, B2B ones in particular, don't really have a clear set of values. Think about a CRM provider, for instance. If you stretch it, one could say their value is in helping people to achieve their sales more comfortably, but this is unlikely to strongly match up well with your personal values.

So, it is true that the positions in the space you want to operate can be scarce. I don't believe there's a simple solution to this but to keep in mind that finding a job that fits your values can take time, dedication, and some luck.

Pressure from Others

In the relaxed world of software engineering, there's still a good deal of social pressure and the achiever mindset. It's often praised when someone climbs the corporate ladder, gets a bigger salary, or works for a prestigious company. There's a status game associated with being a CTO or working for FAANG. But this race for recognition can sometimes get in the way of finding a job that truly means something to you.

Many people pursue the path I've outlined purely for the status it offers, so if it happens that a job aligns with your values and has a high status, the combination can make the competition truly fierce. That's why it's often smart to determine what's more important to you: the status or the sense of purpose you get from your job. Balancing both can be a tough task.

141

Don't See How They Contribute

The final crucial aspect to consider is that not every engineer can easily see their direct contribution to a company's end goal. If you're building a back-office tool for a large corporation focused on increasing lifespan, you might not feel a clear connection to the final outcome. To tackle this issue, it's beneficial to not only understand the mission of the company but also to know what your team will be doing and how closely it aligns with the end result.

Another factor to consider is your individual impact. If you are one of the key players shaping the final result, it usually feels a lot more significant than if you're one of the thousands of developers building the technology. Generally, in smaller companies, software engineers are likely to be closer to their mission and have a more significant impact on the outcome.

Summary

- Working on projects that align with your personal values can lead to higher meaningfulness, job satisfaction, and productivity.

- Identify your values to find the right jobs.

- Focus on the company's mission and values, not just the technology stack, salary, and benefits.

- Choose what is more important to chase—status or purpose. It is hard to get both.

- Figure out how your team and you personally will contribute to the company's mission.

References

[1]   www.betterup.com/blog/work-values

[2]   www.oreilly.com/library/view/the-busy-
        leaders/9781119576648/c30.xhtml#c30-note-0001

CHAPTER 12

Health

Health is the starting point for everything. You can't be productive or feel good if you're constantly exhausted or dealing with a headache, right? For instance, if I don't maintain a healthy diet, take a break from exercise, face a difficult emotional situation, or lack good sleep, my work satisfaction and productivity take a nosedive. During the height of the coronavirus pandemic, I found myself exercising less, eating poorly, and having disruptive sleep patterns. This lifestyle took a toll on me and led me into such a state of frustration and lack of motivation that my doctor suggested I see a psychotherapist for potential depression. At that time, I was about to relocate, so therapy was put on hold. However, after moving to another country, I realized I needed a change. I delved into health-related literature, tried various approaches, and tweaked my routines in numerous ways. When I started properly caring for my sleep, physical activity, nutrition, and mental health, the benefits were soon apparent. I regained my motivation and energy, and within six months, I was feeling even better than before the pandemic. This experience taught me the fundamental importance of health and well-being, and I have maintained these practices ever since.

However, I've noticed that many developers tend to overlook these crucial factors for productivity and well-being. If you find yourself feeling lethargic most of the time, longing for a nap after just two hours of work, or unable to see your knees past your belly, it's probably time to make some life changes.

M. Chernenko, *The Rational Software Engineer*,
https://doi.org/10.1007/978-1-4842-9795-7_12

While I'm not a health professional, I am passionate about this topic, so I have amassed a variety of excellent resources that I'll reference. I'll leave these in the references along with a list of insightful books and podcasts that I follow regularly on this topic [1, 2]. Plus, I'll share my personal practices. And, of course, it's always best to consult with your doctor before starting any new health routines.

Let's dive into the most important areas of well-being by breaking down the key topics one by one: sleep, exercise, nutrition, relationships, psychological care, and other beneficial practices.

Sleep

Good sleep is essential for our adequate functioning [3], while disrupted sleep negatively impacts cognitive performance, and it can lead to fatigue and increased sleepiness [4]. Intriguingly, people often believe they've adapted to light sleep deprivation and maintain their usual cognitive abilities. However, this is not the case as cognitive abilities decrease dramatically with prolonged poor sleep [5]. There are several key elements to achieving high-quality sleep [6, 7]:

- **Consistency**: Maintain a regular sleep schedule, going to bed and waking up at the same time each day, including on weekends.

- **Caffeine**: Avoid caffeine for at least eight to ten hours before going to bed.

- **Alcohol**: Avoid consuming alcohol six hours before going to sleep.

- **Light Exposure**: Minimize exposure to light at least one hour before going to sleep and throughout the night.

- **Morning Sunlight**: Aim to get 30–60 minutes of sunlight exposure shortly after waking up.

- **Temperature**: Consider taking a warm shower before bed and aim to sleep in a cooler environment.

- **Late Dinners**: Don't eat heavy meals two to three hours before bedtime.

Exercise

Current guidelines recommend at least 75 minutes of vigorous physical activity per week or 150 minutes of moderate-intensity activity per week [8]. In addition, strength training and high-intensity interval training (HIIT) are beneficial and have been shown to improve cognitive performance [9]. Moreover, there are two types of cardio that significantly improved my energy levels as described in the book, *Outlive* [1]:

- **Endurance Jogging**: Incorporate two one-hour jogs per week at a pace that makes speaking somewhat challenging.

- **Interval Running**: This involves alternating between high and low intensity. A session could include four rounds of four-minute high-speed running followed by four minutes of slow-paced running. This workout aims to improve your VO_2 max, which is a measure of your body's ability to use oxygen.

So in total, I do strength training three times per week for about 45 minutes each, and I do two runs for about 90 minutes in total.

Nutrition

The field of nutrition has fierce ongoing debates about which diet is superior. As highlighted in "Outlive," it's difficult to definitively say which among the many healthy diets is best. The challenges lie in conducting lifelong studies in this area, so currently, there isn't a comprehensive meta-study to answer this question. However, it's generally agreed upon that certain dietary choices are detrimental to health.

One trend that's universally accepted is the need to avoid the Standard American Diet (SAD), which is characterized by high amounts of processed foods, refined carbohydrates and added sugars, refined fats, and high-fat dairy products. Beyond that, a few key points to consider include the following:

1. **Glucose Spikes**: Glucose spikes are undesirable. While individuals may react differently to various foods, it's generally accepted that "fast" carbohydrates or refined sugars cause rapid spikes in blood glucose levels. On the other hand, slow carbohydrates, reducing caloric intake, intermittent fasts, and consuming sugars around exercise time can help moderate these spikes.

2. **Protein Intake**: Ensure you're getting enough protein—at least 0.8g per kg of your weight [10]. "Outlive" suggests a higher intake, recommending 2.2g per kg or 1g per pound of body weight to keep muscle mass as we age.

3. **Healthy Fats**: Include healthy fats in your diet. Opt for foods rich in beneficial fats such as extra virgin olive oil, avocados, and nuts. Conversely, reduce intake of butter, lard, and omega-6-rich oils like corn, soybean, and sunflower.

4. **Essential Nutrients**: Aim to get a variety of essential nutrients, including vitamins and minerals, from different food sources. There are also different supplements that can provide these in comfortable form, which can be of help if you struggle to maintain a healthy diet. I tried AG1, and it seems to cover pretty a lot from the list of essential nutrients.

5. **Microbiome Health**: Both fermented foods and fiber are beneficial for maintaining a healthy microbiome, which is important for overall digestion and health [11].

6. **Vitamin D**: Our bodies need about 600 IU of vitamin D each day. We primarily obtain this nutrient through sun exposure, but during seasons or situations where adequate sunlight isn't available, such as in winter, supplementation might be necessary [12].

Remember, these guidelines are broad, and individual nutritional needs may vary.

Relationships

Maintaining positive, fulfilling relationships is an essential aspect of overall well-being. A healthy romantic relationship has been strongly associated with increased happiness, self-esteem, safety, and life satisfaction [13]. Friendships play a significant role as well; robust social connections have been linked to lower risks of heart disease, reduced stress levels, and improved mental health [14].

This understanding leads me to prioritize surrounding myself with good people to maintain a satisfactory overall state. It's all too easy to drift away from social circles and meaningful interactions if no effort is put into maintaining them. Thus, I consciously set aside time for social activities each week when planning my schedule.

Psychological Care

Psychological care is a broad topic that extends beyond the scope of a single subsection. However, I'd like to briefly highlight a few essential elements for further exploration.

We all encounter significant stress at times, making it vital to learn effective stress management techniques. Deep, slow breathing can be an effective tool, reducing stress and anxiety by slowing the heart rate and lowering blood pressure [15]. It's a simple technique that can provide immediate relief from stress. Another popular method is mindfulness, a slightly more challenging practice to master, yet highly effective in combating stress and anxiety [16]. I personally enjoy doing five-minute sessions of slow breathing for relaxation.

Mindfulness meditation isn't the only beneficial type of meditation; numerous techniques can be helpful here [17]. For instance, concentrative meditation improves overall focus [18], while loving-kindness meditation (metta) can enhance positivity, empathy, and compassionate behavior toward others [19]. I do 20 minutes of mindfulness meditation per day with the Waking Up app.

Lastly, I'd like to emphasize the value of psychotherapy. I think this aspect is especially important as I meet so many people who struggle with burnout or depression in our field. As well as that, challenges outside of work such as relationship struggles, addiction, or grief can adversely affect our concentration and performance at work. All of these can be effectively treated with psychotherapy.

Psychotherapy comes in different forms such as cognitive behavior therapy, which can help reshape thoughts and feelings around specific topics, or EMDR (eye movement desensitization and reprocessing), which is effective in dealing with traumatic events [20]. Importantly, therapy isn't solely beneficial for those grappling with severe mental issues. Whether you're confronting substantial challenges or minor hurdles in your life, psychotherapy can provide significant relief; even a single session can sometimes make a difference [21]. For a comprehensive guide on psychotherapy, its potential benefits, and tips on choosing a therapist, I recommend referring to this resource [21]. I personally have sought the assistance of a psychotherapist to help manage my social anxiety and gain a deeper perspective on the smaller issues in my life. Therapy is also my place to get new insights about my life and behavior that are harder to notice on my own.

Other Practices

Drawing from a series of videos on longevity, Dr. David Sinclair suggests that small, controlled stressors, a concept known as "hormesis," can actually be beneficial to our bodies as they promote resilience [22]. This category encompasses practices such as intermittent fasting and exposure to cold and heat.

In these guides [23, 24], you'll find more comprehensive information about the various protocols and health benefits associated with cold and heat exposure. Personally, I aim to incorporate one to two cold showers or baths per week, each lasting three to ten minutes. These sessions are intended to boost my focus, motivation, and immune system. Additionally, I engage in one to two sauna sessions each week, with temperatures ranging from 80°C to 120°C for a duration of 20 minutes. This practice aims to enhance mood, strengthen heart health, and provide overall health benefits.

Summary

Don't simply take my word for it. I encourage you to dive deeper into the topic of health, conduct your own research, test different strategies, and discover what suits you best. You'll likely see an improvement in your ability to handle work stress and challenges and an overall boost in your happiness.

To recap, here are the main health-enhancing practices I've highlighted in this chapter:

- **Sleep**: Maintain a consistent sleep schedule, avoid caffeine and alcohol close to bedtime, limit light exposure before sleep, get morning sunlight exposure, and keep your sleeping environment cool.

- **Exercise**: Engage in at least 75 minutes of vigorous or 150 minutes of moderate-intensity physical activity per week, including strength training or high-intensity interval training (HIIT).

- **Nutrition**: Avoid diets high in refined sugars and unhealthy fats, ensure sufficient protein intake, consume a variety of essential nutrients, prioritize foods that promote a healthy microbiome, and consider vitamin D supplementation if necessary.

- **Relationships**: Prioritize time for maintaining and nurturing positive relationships as they contribute significantly to overall well-being and stress reduction.

- **Psychological Care**: Utilize stress management techniques such as deep, slow breathing and mindfulness, consider different forms of meditation for various benefits, and don't hesitate to seek professional help such as psychotherapy if needed.

- **Other Practices**: Engage in "hormesis" practices such as intermittent fasting and exposure to cold and heat for their various health benefits.

References

[1]   Overall healthspan guide, www.amazon.com/Outlive-Longevity-Peter-Attia-MD/dp/0593236599

[2]   A podcast about neurobiology and health, https://hubermanlab.com/

[3]   Importance of sleep, Why We Sleep www.amazon.com/Why-We-Sleep-Unlocking-Dreams/dp/1501144316

[4]   Sleep quality, duration, and consistency are associated with better academic performance in college students, www.nature.com/articles/s41539-019-0055-z

[5]   How Does Lack of Sleep Affect Cognitive Impairment, www.sleepfoundation.org/sleep-deprivation/lack-of-sleep-and-cognitive-impairment

[6]   Toolkit for sleep, https://hubermanlab.com/toolkit-for-sleep/

[7]   Sleep protocols, www.masterclass.com/articles/matthew-walker-on-improving-sleep-quality

[8]   Physical Activity Guidelines for Americans, https://health.gov/our-work/nutrition-physical-activity/physical-activity-guidelines

[9]   High-Intensity Interval Training upon Cognitive
         and Psychological Outcomes in Youth: A Systematic
         Review, https://pubmed.ncbi.nlm.nih.
         gov/34067861/

[10]   How much protein do you need every day?, www.
         health.harvard.edu/blog/how-much-protein-do-
         you-need-every-day-201506188096

[11]   6 Key Tools to Improve Your Gut Microbiome Health,
         https://hubermanlab.com/6-key-tools-to-improve-
         your-gut-microbiome-health/

[12]   Vitamin D, www.mayoclinic.org/drugs-supplements-
         vitamin-d/art-20363792

[13]   Well-Being and Romantic Relationships: A Systematic
         Review in Adolescence and Emerging Adulthood, www.
         ncbi.nlm.nih.gov/pmc/articles/PMC6650954/

[14]   The Health Benefits of Strong Relationships, www.
         health.harvard.edu/staying-healthy/the-health-
         benefits-of-strong-relationships

[15]   This Slow-Breathing Exercise Can Reduce Stress and
         Anxiety, www.psychologytoday.com/us/blog/urban-
         survival/202204/slow-breathing-exercise-can-
         reduce-stress-and-anxiety

[16]   Mindfulness meditation: A research-proven way to
         reduce stress, www.apa.org/topics/mindfulness/
         meditation

[17]   How Meditation Impacts Your Mind and Body, www.
         verywellmind.com/what-is-meditation-2795927

[18]   Meditation Can Improve Concentration,
       https://content.time.com/time/health/
       article/0,8599,2008914,00.html

[19]   Benefits of Meditation: 12 Science-Based Benefits of
       Meditation, www.healthline.com/nutrition/12-
       benefits-of-meditation

[20]   Trauma Therapy: Definition, Types, Techniques,
       and Efficacy, www.verywellmind.com/trauma-
       therapy-definition-types-techniques-and-
       efficacy-5191413

[21]   Understanding psychotherapy and how it works, www.
       apa.org/topics/psychotherapy/understanding

[22]   The Science Behind Why We Age, www.youtube.com/
       watch?v=X1kLizzdb2c

[23]   Using Deliberate Cold Exposure for Health and
       Performance, https://hubermanlab.com/using-
       deliberate-cold-exposure-for-health-and-
       performance/

[24]   Deliberate Heat Exposure Protocols for Health &
       Performance, https://hubermanlab.com/deliberate-
       heat-exposure-protocols-for-health-and-
       performance/

CHAPTER 13

Company Attitude

Our perception of our employer and the overall company directly influences our collaboration level and attitude toward the company's happenings. If we handle our managers, other teams, or the company itself with negligence or outright hostility, it can rebound negatively on our motivation and performance. Therefore, let's initially discuss the drawbacks of the "us vs. them" mindset within teams, interteams or departments, management, and the company at large and then explore strategies to foster a positive attitude.

Teams

In the realm of teams, the "us vs. them" mentality often takes root when we try to find "enemies" within our team. This mentality follows with a negative attitude toward some people who are external to your group and blaming them for being the cause of a lot of problems, which they actually are not responsible for. The most interesting part is that most often, the "enemies" have the same goal as the "us."

A common example I've noticed is the tendency for the quality assurance team to be seen as an "enemy" by the engineering team. This attitude becomes evident when a developer rolls their eyes and mutters, "Not again," upon receiving a bug report from QA. This scenario is particularly amusing, considering both roles, engineers and QA, are aiming for the same outcome: the production of high-quality software.

M. Chernenko, *The Rational Software Engineer*,
https://doi.org/10.1007/978-1-4842-9795-7_13

Another frequent case involves confrontation with a designer or product manager. They might emphasize other crucial aspects of development and seem to fail to fully grasp the importance and complexity of building software from a technical perspective. In reality, they're offering a different viewpoint that needs to be merged with ours to create a comprehensive picture. The team should aim to strike a balance between technical feasibility and elegance, feature value, and user experience. Typically, achieving this equilibrium requires compromises from all parties involved, as it should.

A useful approach to battle this mentality is to continually remind ourselves that we all share the same objective: to create a high-quality, bug-free, and user-friendly product. If anyone forgets this shared purpose or if emotions start interfering, it becomes crucial to reassert that everyone is collaboratively working toward this common goal.

Interteams and Departments

Different teams and departments within a company can often have varying goals and at times; there may be a natural tendency to compete with one another. When these goals are seriously misaligned, it usually requires management intervention to resolve such issues. For instance, I once worked at a place where we were aiming to automate the onboarding and trial start process, a departure from the manual sales process we had been using. While this seemed like a beneficial change, it actually reduced the number of sales required for the company to operate. Despite the sales team being professional and understanding, it was only natural that they weren't entirely supportive or pleased with this shift. In situations like these, I find that management can assist by reorganizing the way teams collaborate and by devising a plan that benefits everyone involved. In this case, it could be by offering sales personnel additional bonuses for a quick transition to the new automated system and providing them with the new tasks they will have once they migrate, so they are confident in their job security and the opportunity to take on interesting work within the company.

However, there are also times when competition and tension arise without any apparent reason. Teams may start off on the wrong foot when they begin to collaborate. For example, while I was part of a team developing support authorization features for other teams, one team didn't participate during the requirements gathering phase for our system but then suddenly reappeared when we were making a monthly priority plan. They strongly insisted on implementing a feature that only their team needed within the next week or two, which messed up our plans and other important priorities. This did not create a cooperative atmosphere. Still, it's essential to remember that such issues often stem from somewhere. I later discovered that this team was being pressured by their management, who in turn was being pushed by a critical client of our company. In the end, the issue was more about poor communication rather than anyone being at fault, and we were able to clarify and resolve it in due course.

Manager

The "us vs. them" mentality often intensifies when it comes to management. Occasionally, they'll make decisions you won't agree with, and understanding their rationale may be difficult.

However, with some empathy, it becomes easier to comprehend that managers are just people who deal with their own challenges. They might make decisions we find hard to relate to due to several factors, such as their own inexperience and potential mistakes (just like the ones any of us could make), or due to the context of which we might not be aware. Managers play a critical role, acting as an umbrella to protect us from irrelevant or even disruptive information that could distract the team's focus, and they strive to represent our interests in the best way they can, both of which I am deeply appreciative of. Furthermore, it's usually the managers who bear the weight of the responsibility if a project fails, making them the ones who usually endure the most stress.

It's important to remember that they share the same fundamental goal with you—to ensure the project's success within the given budget or other constraints. Maintaining healthy relationships with them fosters more effective collaboration toward this common goal and also provides you with a deeper understanding of the reasoning behind their decisions.

Company

The most challenging entity to connect with in the whole hierarchy is often the company itself. You might feel that the corporate structures impose certain solutions and limit our freedom to do what we're good at, such as writing code. The situation becomes even more complex when your values do not align with the company's mission.

Though it may not always be apparent, the company's goals and your own are generally aligned. Both you and the company want growth and profitability. These objectives allow the company to sustain and expand its staff, which ensures job security for you.

Summary

The "us vs. them" mindset can occur at various levels within a company, but it's not beneficial for anybody involved. It's important to remember that despite seeming differences, your team and the entire organization usually share the same overall objective, so fostering collaboration and alignment is key.

CHAPTER 14

Handling Failures

I fail a lot, my assumptions turn out to be wrong, my judgments and predictions may be completely incorrect, my estimates fail, and I produce bugs. It's the essence of software engineering to try and fail, so there is nothing to be ashamed of.

Curiosity Always Leads to Mistakes

We've discussed before how curiosity plays a key role in learning. One aspect of curiosity is that it can lead to moments where you realize your understanding was incorrect, and in fact, when people make mistakes during learning, they learn better [1]. So it's crucial to have the humility to accept when you've made a mistake and learn from it. There's no shame in making mistakes; in fact, the only shame is in claiming that you've never made a mistake.

For instance, I used to think that WebSockets operate over two UDP connections because there's no application-level acknowledgment of messages. But I was totally wrong; WebSockets actually use a single TCP connection. I also remember a discussion where I told a groupmate it was impossible to create an asynchronous engine with just one thread, as JavaScript does. It seemed impossible until I read about how Futures work in Rust [1], which explains how to do it using one thread with help from an IO-aware system blocking tool like Linux's epoll.

© Mykyta Chernenko 2023
M. Chernenko, *The Rational Software Engineer*,
https://doi.org/10.1007/978-1-4842-9795-7_14

Sometimes, trying something new like introducing a new tool to a project, a new process to a team, or giving a public tech speech can be scary. We are all afraid to seem incompetent, stupid, and shortsighted. But at the same time, there is no more powerful approach to learning than trying something out. So it's important to embrace that you can and will fail constantly in this long journey.

How to Handle Failures

The variety of mistakes you can make is vast, and each type requires different skills to handle and accept.

If you make a minor slipup, like saying that subroutines cannot take less memory than threads, the only thing hurt is your ego. But it's essential to remember that an ego-driven stance seldom leads to positive outcomes. I've seen developers engage in lengthy disputes about system design simply because one of them was too proud to admit their solution was not the best fit as he forgot about the cold start time of AWS Lambda. This sort of high ego stance isn't beneficial for anybody involved. It slows learning, discourages feedback, and often leads to conversations centered more on protecting egos than solving problems. It's crucial to recognize when your ego is influencing your actions and ensure it doesn't hinder your growth and affect others negatively.

However, some mistakes are harder to accept and require more courage to take responsibility for. For instance, it's tough to admit fault for a production server failure that cost the company money and led to the loss of some clients. But owning up to such mistakes is the right thing to do. The role of a good software engineer involves taking responsibility, especially when it comes to failures. When things go wrong, it's human nature to avoid blame. Yet, most of the time, management isn't interested in pointing fingers; they want to understand how to prevent such issues in the future because they don't want to lose money and customers again. And they're used to people avoiding responsibility. So, when someone steps up and says, "Yes, our team didn't have a robust enough process in place to detect downtimes in our payment provider. We're now devising steps to improve this, so it either won't happen again, or we'll get notified and can resolve it quicker," they prove to be a valuable asset for management. This ownership not only displays the right attitude and firm character but is also highly appreciated.

Others' Failures

It's worth mentioning that the same mindset should be applied to people that surround you. There is no person who doesn't make mistakes, your manager, mentor, or role model included. Sometimes it may seem that the mistakes they made were obvious to avoid. However, it's always easy to judge from hindsight.

There is a very good example from my experience that still gives me a little bit of shivering down my spine each time I recall it. When I worked on my project at university in my second year, I needed persistent storage to deploy my Django application on Heroku. I had zero knowledge about clouds at that time, and I needed to find something that was quick to integrate with, cheap, or, even better, free. A lot of guides pointed toward using S3. If you remember your first exposure to AWS, I think, you understand how lost one can feel. I needed to simply create storage for my images, but I had to go through tons of concepts and configurations. In the end, not having been able to get all of the concepts, I used my Admin API Key to access the S3 and pushed the key right to my public GitHub repo. The next day I saw a star on my GitHub repo from a person I didn't know and a bill for $3000 for using GPU-optimized EC2 instances. One crypto miner apparently enjoyed using my AWS Admin API Keys.

After that, I try not to judge others and remind myself of tons of stupid failures that I've done myself. Instead, I try to give others space to fail and learn and chime in when my guidance is helpful.

Summary

Keep in mind that handling failure is also a measure of your character. When you accept failure and learn from it, you become more resilient and equipped for future challenges. This process nurtures your perseverance in difficult times and enhances your growth as a software engineer. Acknowledging that you and others will make mistakes is vital. So stay open to accepting failure and taking responsibility for it.

References

[1]   Making mistakes while studying actually helps
        you learn better, `www.sciencedaily.com/`
        `releases/2018/06/180611133437.htm`

[2]   Executors and System IO - Asynchronous
        Programming in Rust, `https://rust-lang.github.io/`
        `async-book/02_execution/05_io.html`

PART III

Learning

As I stressed in Chapter 9, "Lifelong Learning," it's essential to keep learning in the fast-changing field of Software Engineering. With technology always changing, professionals need to stay updated and seek new knowledge constantly. But simply knowing that you need to learn is not enough. In this part, we'll immerse into the world of learning, discussing both what to learn and the best ways to go about it. Here is the outline of the chapters we are going to cover:

> **Chapter 15, "What to Learn"**: The journey begins with identifying what areas to focus on. We'll discuss the dual-edged sword of specializing in one area, the significance of diversifying skills, and the importance of choosing the right learning resources—ranging from fundamental books to universities. Conferences, courses, and other avenues will also be emphasized as powerful learning tools.

> **Chapter 16, "Learning Effectively"**: Once you've decided what to learn, the next step is mastering how to learn. Effective learning isn't just about absorbing information, but about integrating it. I will describe techniques like dedicated timeslots, learning by practice, note-taking, and leveraging tools like ChatGPT.

Chapter 17, "Feedback": Feedback is a two-way street. We'll delve into the art and science of giving constructive feedback and the value of feedback directed at you.

Chapter 18, "Learning from Other People": Not all knowledge comes from books or courses; much can be learned from human interaction. From seeking mentorship (both official and unofficial) to understanding the dynamics of pair programming, this chapter outlines the importance of interpersonal learning channels.

Chapter 19, "Sharing Your Knowledge": The cycle of learning is incomplete without sharing your knowledge. We'll look into how sharing one's knowledge—through in-company seminars, conferences, writing, or mentoring—can not only benefit others but also deepen your own understanding.

Chapter 20, "Learning from Code": Diving into code bases, understanding documentation, and leveraging techniques like skimming will be covered here, emphasizing the core skills that every engineer should harness to make the most of every line of code they encounter.

Chapter 21, "Rotation": Lastly, the concept of rotation, its pros and cons, and its significance in broadening an engineer's horizons will be addressed.

CHAPTER 15

What to Learn

We've discussed the importance of continuous learning and improvement as a software engineer. But simply learning for the sake of learning isn't sufficient. It's crucial to focus on learning the right things. So, let's look into how we can make wise decisions on what to invest our time in, in both careerwise and short-term contexts.

To Focus on One Thing or Not

When you think about your career and what you need to learn, there are two main paths: deep specialization or being a generalist. Deep specialization means focusing all your efforts on one area. For example, if TypeScript is popular, you'd spend most of your time becoming an expert in TypeScript, tracking all the "nightly" versions, going to TypeScript-specific conferences, and only looking for jobs within the TypeScript realm.

On the other hand, being a generalist means you learn a bit of everything. You might study TypeScript, have Python in your side project, and sometimes read about what's new in Rust. This way, you know a bit about many tools without typically being an expert in any of them.

Both ways can work, and it really depends on what you prefer. But it's important to know how they can affect your job prospects and how to avoid problems.

© Mykyta Chernenko 2023
M. Chernenko, *The Rational Software Engineer*,
https://doi.org/10.1007/978-1-4842-9795-7_15

With deep specialization, you often have a better chance when a company is looking for someone with your specific skills. For example, if a company's systems are all built in Java and they plan to keep it that way, someone with nine years of Java experience is usually more attractive than someone with a mix of Java, Python, and Go experience. Also, without deep specialization, you might find it challenging to participate in cutting-edge "cool" technology, such as robotic dogs used for industrial safety monitoring. I faced this reality as a generalist when I applied for such a position. I was overlooked in favor of a candidate with a degree in robotics and more IoT experience. Even though that person might have had less overall experience and other expertise, they had a clear advantage: they already had all the specific knowledge needed for that particular role. I, on the other hand, would have had to learn as I went along. And this contemplation is something that every employee does when they hire a generalist vs. specialist.

Having a lot of pros, being a specialist can also cause problems if, for example, demand for your technology choice drops. While sometimes there's a boost in demand for old technology, like Cobol or PHP, because lots of old systems need to be maintained, usually when technology becomes less popular, demand for it plummets, and you can't find a new job. Also, if you focus too much on one technology, you might struggle to pick up new things because the skill to learn drastically new information typically slowly degrades when you learn only around specific tech. So, if you decide to be a specialist, it's still a good idea to learn a bit about other technologies and keep an eye on what's happening in the wider tech world.

If you're a generalist, it's usually easier to get a job in smaller, more flexible companies as they often have a "pragmatic" attitude to their tech stack and are looking for someone who can do a bit of everything. And it's still a good idea to have one technology that you're really good at, so if you can't find a generalist job, you can look for a job where your main skill is needed.

Now let's talk more about how to and what to learn.

Self-Learning

Usually, there's no set schedule or regular assessment of our learning progress. At most, we might get an annual performance review that briefly touches on our development and growth. This means that the most immediate feedback we might get from not staying updated is facing challenges while seeking a new job, and that could be years to come.

The primary drive for self-learning comes from recognizing its importance. Being a competent software engineer largely depends on continuous learning. However, encouraging yourself to learn consistently can be tough without additional motivation. Things like deadlines, obligations, and group responsibilities can act as good additional motivators, and we'll dive into how to use these later.

So, the big question is, when you're setting out to learn on your own, how do you decide where to focus?

Choosing Topics

As a software engineer, there's an endless list of topics to learn. However, I concentrate on subjects that will benefit my role the most:

- **Directly Job-Related Topics**: I prioritize learning about topics immediately relevant to my job that I'm not yet familiar with. For instance, if I start a project that requires SpringBoot, and I have no experience with it, I'll prioritize learning SpringBoot. The same approach applies to future changes in my project; like if we plan to create a microservice in the functional paradigm next month using Elixir, I need to read up on it.

- **Company-Wide Relevant Topics**: I also focus on topics that are relevant across the company. If other teams use certain technologies, understanding them can help me grasp the system as a whole. Say, if an identity team uses Auth0 or an infrastructure team introduces Kafka for company-wide data sharing, I'll learn these to enhance my overall tech understanding and potentially contribute to or switch to those teams. Also, nonengineering domain knowledge topics also fall into this category. For example, if your company operates in the tendering industry, it's worth reading up on different aspects of tendering so that you have a good basic understanding of the domain.

- **Commonly Known Topics**: It's useful to understand what others around me know and I don't to establish a common ground and find obvious knowledge gaps. For example, if everyone discusses network table configurations during the stand-up and I struggle with understanding network masks, it's a clear signal I need to learn about them.

- **Fundamental Understanding**: Understanding the main concepts that drive technology is highly beneficial as it is often transferable to other specific technologies. A good understanding of a binary tree, for example, could help to grasp how binary search, database indexes, and substring search problems work. Also, a deep understanding of OOP patterns is transferable between languages. For example, if a project I'm involved in uses an ML model, knowing its architecture, however basic, helps me understand its limitations and how to best use and scale it, so I will prioritize learning it.

- **Development Efficiency**: I value topics that can speed up my development. A shortcut saving 5 seconds per use and used 50 times a day can save a significant amount of work over time. Good project, debug, autocompletion setup, and new productivity also fall into this category.

- **Trending Concepts**: As I mentioned, keeping up-to-date with trending concepts in the field is enjoyable and potentially beneficial for future employment.

- **Paradigm-Challenging Concepts**: It's beneficial to learn concepts that counter my typical paradigm. If I favor SQL, it's worth learning about No-SQL databases. If I prefer compiled, strongly typed languages, I might explore something dynamic and loosely typed.

- **Nontechnical, Broad Topics**: Topics like product management, client communication, and UX techniques, while nontechnical, offer a broader perspective of the business as a whole.

- **Soft Skills Improvement**: Improving soft skills is an area of focus as well, and it aids a variety of other tasks and enhances different aspects of my career.

- **Recommendations**: If somebody with good expertise recommends reading material, I typically add it to my list as well.

Good Education Guide

When I'm learning about a broad topic where my knowledge is limited or know that a topic is big and I will study it for a while, I often turn to education guides. These guides offer a structured path and thorough understanding if followed correctly. I'm a fan of guides like roadmap. sh, which outlines a clear learning journey for various tech specialties. I leaned on it when diving deeper into architecture and often recommend it to trainees and juniors I mentor. With such a guide, you're less likely to get overwhelmed and more likely to know your next step.

Education guides come in different shapes. They can be courses, mentoring sessions, or even university programs. What they all have in common is guiding the learner through a structured knowledge journey. Now, let's delve into various educational resources and their pros and cons.

Newsletter and Blogs

As a software engineer, one challenge is keeping up with our ever-changing knowledge. What was relevant two years ago might be obsolete today. For instance, using GPT in 2023 for coding with something as fluid as JavaScript libraries or DevOps tools works pretty poorly half of the time as it was trained on pre-2021 data, and it doesn't know about all the breaking changes, new features, tools, and approaches that have happened since. It's like a professional who hasn't updated their skills in a few years.

Traditional learning sources like universities, courses, and books can become outdated quickly. Hence, it's essential to have resources that keep us current. Newsletters and blogs are great for this. Subscribing to a handful of newsletters can keep you informed about weekly or monthly industry changes. And platforms like Medium or Hackernoon consistently offer fresh technical articles.

I could share my current go-to list, but given how fast things change, it might be outdated in a year. So, I'd suggest finding a few article websites and newsletters that align with your goals and always be on the lookout for new good resources here.

At the same time, some newsletters and articles can be filled with hype. They can grab a lot of attention, but sometimes they only show a narrow or biased view of a topic. Take AI as an example: many AI companies launch every year. But if a well-known person starts an AI company, that's the only one you might see in a newsletter for a month. Because of this, I tend to view these hype-driven newsletters like regular news. I skim through, looking for what's worth a deeper read.

Now let's jump to something more fundamental: books.

Books

Books are sometimes skipped by software engineers, but since you're here, I guess we both see their worth. A well-organized book can offer an in-depth look at a topic, point to further information, and share techniques useful across different areas.

There are many books focused on specific topics. For example, *SpringBoot/Kotlin/JavaScript in Action*, edition 17 dives into one or a combination of technologies. I find such detailed books especially handy when

- You're switching to a new project and need a deep guide on an unfamiliar tech stack.

- You're at the start of your career aiming to gain expertise in a field.

- You're aiming to expand a specialization you're already deep into.

For other situations, I lean more toward books that share knowledge usable in many contexts. For example, a book about networking and its protocols can be used in many ways, while one about new Go features has a narrower focus. There are some truly standout books on a range of topics. Below, I've listed some top reads I enjoyed, with brief descriptions:

- **Code Complete** by Steve McConnell: This is a classic and my top pick on software engineering. It offers various techniques and is packed with useful statistics in the relevant sections.

- **The Pragmatic Programmer** by Andy Hunt and Dave Thomas: A valuable book that covers the software engineer's mindset and a range of useful day-to-day techniques.

- **500 Lines or Less** by various open source authors: This insightful book presents the design concepts behind several open source projects with thorough explanations.

- **Clean Code** by Uncle Bob: This is another essential read that gives hands-on guidance on writing better code, especially for those at an intermediate level.

- **Design Patterns** by Gang of Four: This book lays out the most frequently used design patterns in object-oriented programming. There's a similar version on the website refactoring.guru by a different author.

- **Refactoring** by Martin Fowler: A comprehensive guide on standard refactoring methods. You can find similar content on refactoring.guru.

- **The Manager's Path** by Camille Fournier: This serves as a solid starting point for those aiming at a Tech Lead or higher managerial role. However, if you're already experienced, it might feel basic.

- **The Product Book** by Carlos González de Villaumbrosia: A thorough introduction to the realm of product management.

- **From Zero to One** by Blake Masters and Peter Thiel: A good and interesting take on what is needed to build a startup and how to do it best.

University

The significance of a higher degree for software engineers is a deeply debated topic. Some argue its inefficiency, stating that it's outdated and redundant, labeling it a waste of time and effort. Meanwhile, others see it as essential and often condescend to those without a degree. They emphasize the structured information, networking opportunities, and the overall enhancement it provides to one's skills.

My perspective is in the middle. Universities undeniably offer a structured approach to fundamental knowledge, which can be challenging to attain later, such as algorithms, deep dives into computer science, networking, databases, and more. The connections you make could become valuable references or lifelong friends. It's not uncommon for university connections to lead to your first job or, at the very least, simplify the job search after graduation. Additionally, a higher degree can be a key to unlocking opportunities as some companies and visa processes require formal education.

However, there's another side. Committing years to study before truly experiencing the field is an inefficient method to understand if it's the right fit. Thus, gaining real-world experience early on during university years, either through internships or better yet, part-time jobs, is invaluable. It offers a more immersive experience. The quality of university education can also be inconsistent. Not all lecturers will be on the cutting edge or possess the skills to share their knowledge effectively. And there are some subjects that are required in some universities but have very little direct knowledge impact on what you will know as a software engineer: philosophy, advanced mathematics, physics, and many more. There's a high chance some lectures will be a poor investment of time.

But let's say that you have a bachelor's and some years of work experience in your bag. And now you consider whether it is a good decision to go for a master's. If it's in the same field you have experience with and you don't lean toward scientific research, it might not be the best use of your time. While we learn a lot of computer **science**, the practical aspects lean more toward craftsmanship, which is much better taught in the process. I'd pursue further studies only if they offer concrete benefits or simply for the joy of learning.

Courses

Courses are a shorter, focused alternative to university, making them an excellent choice for beginners. They allow you to dive into a subject, practice it, and then test the waters in a job market to see if the field truly resonates with you.

Courses offer great flexibility. If you begin one and realize it's not what you expected, you can simply switch to a different course due to its short duration. This makes it easier to find the best learning experience adapted to your needs.

Courses are also valuable for more experienced individuals. If you're looking to deepen your knowledge in a particular area or consider a slight career change, a course can offer structured learning without a huge time commitment.

Moreover, if you're hesitant about enrolling in a full-time university program, another option, which resembles a course, is to attend select university classes. This way, you can benefit from the most useful content without committing to a complete degree program.

Conferences

Many people see conferences as a useful place for further education, and there's some truth to that. You can spend a few days soaking up insights from industry experts on the matter that is relevant to you.

However, I've found this format isn't always the most effective for deep learning. With just 30–60 minutes for each session, there's limited depth a speaker can go into. Plus, with diverse audiences, content often gets generalized to cater to everyone. As a result, conferences often give just a taste of a topic without the meaty details. Out of the 50 conference talks I've attended, only a handful were truly impactful. Watching recorded sessions online at my own pace often proves more beneficial.

But conferences aren't just about the presentations. They offer a chance to connect and network. It's not always easy finding peers who share your exact passion or expertise. Conferences bring those people together. So, I'd view them more as valuable networking and social opportunities rather than pure educational events.

Search and LLMs

Search engines aren't just for finding answers; they help us learn too. When I search for something, I often find more than just what I am looking for. Like on StackOverflow, I don't just copy answers. I try to understand the whole thing, which is often provided if you read the answers fully. This process is the same with tools like GPT and other LLMs: they give answers, but it's always better to also ask GPT for a full explanation to really understand a topic.

I really like using GPT. It can adapt its explanations to the style I prefer, give good examples, and use simple comparisons. I think of it as a great guide for learning. And there are many prompts and templates on how to make it even better for learning new material you can find online turning it into a personalized interactive tutor.

Summary

- **Generalist vs. Specialist**: Choose between gaining versatile skills or diving deep into a specific domain, but mitigate the risk of both.

- **Self-Learning**: Recognize the importance of self-learning and learn how to do it correctly.

- **Learning Guide**: Guides can be very useful for structured learning.

- **Newsletters/Blogs**: Stay updated with industry trends and best practices.

- **Books**: Choose books with transferable knowledge or hands-on ones when you learn something new.

- **University**: A huge and not always efficient time investment but provides fundamental knowledge and an easier career journey.

- **Courses**: Flexible learning path with a shorter feedback loop.

- **Conferences**: Great for networking and industry trends, less for in-depth learning.

- **Search**: Learn after you find an answer.

- **GPT**: Use as a great free tutor for any topic that adapts to your style.

CHAPTER 16

Learning Effectively

We all learn in one way or another. We are bombarded with new information that is little but resides in our memory. We may read an article here and there, or we may chat with colleagues about something, but it does not seem effective. Most of the learned or discussed facts disappear from our brains in a week or two. But there are good strategies how to maximize the benefit of learning.

Dedicated Time Slots

Scheduling dedicated uninterrupted time to learn is essential. Multitasking and interruption diminish [1] our ability to learn and make memories, as well as it is fairly easy to skip a week or two at work without any dedicated hours spent on learning. Therefore, I tend to book at least one hour per week in my calendar solemnly responsible for learning new material. For the new beginners, I find it even more important because learning is the main activity, so you and others should treat it as important as "job" time, which is not to be interrupted or replaced with a low-priority activity.

Learn by Practice

By far, practicing is the most important tool to improve the learning process. Actively practicing what you read enhances how much we remember and can after [2]. Development is an amazing field because we

© Mykyta Chernenko 2023
M. Chernenko, *The Rational Software Engineer*,
https://doi.org/10.1007/978-1-4842-9795-7_16

have the opportunity to exercise almost all the technical knowledge that we learn quickly and cheaply.

When I start a course to learn something, I stick to those that provide a way to interactively run my code or with which I can open my terminal side by side and execute the things that are taught. I understand that purely reading theory is mostly useless if I want to integrate the knowledge into my active memory, so I need to always try it with my hands.

When I read a book about a new language, I prefer those that have tasks at the end of each chapter or those that have instructions on how to try out the subject being discussed in code.

When I'm using a new library or a tool, I find it more educational and easier to poke around the library on my own and read the bits in the documentation that I do not understand rather than going through all the documentation first. And it became easier as I gained more overall experience in development.

Also, when I need to use a new tool, I often read only as much as I need to complete the task because I understand that if I do not have time to play around with other things I read, it is wasted time.

At times, there are indeed theoretical materials that have no reasonable chance to be exercised, for example, differences between L1, L2, and L3 cache or opinion or experience-based articles about how to build architecture. For such things, it is important to come back to the learned material.

Recite

Coming back to the notes you've written and the material you've read greatly enhances how much you will remember [3]. And in order to find the forgetting curve [4], which is a fancy term to describe that we gradually forget what we learn, we need to use spatial learning, which means revisiting the learning material gradually increasing offsets between the revisions.

There is no definitive answer as to what the best time gap to use in space learning to revisit the content is as learning a word in a foreign language is different from trying to remember an architecture pattern that you read five pages about and tried to implement in your code, but common techniques include revisiting the material after one day, three days, one week, three weeks, three months, and a year. I tend to revisit the summary of what I learned from articles in a week, month, and year.

Another important thing is to rephrase the things you have learned and explain them to somebody else. This can be used when taking notes, doing knowledge sharing in the company on the topics you learned, mentoring somebody, or speaking to a colleague or a rubber duck. All of this is a form of reciting that will help you to solidify the material in your memory.

Take Notes

To effectively revisit things we learn, we need to create high-quality notes for them. We want to create notes in such a way that they are easily discoverable, there is a reminder to recite them, and we can connect dots between different knowledge pieces for the association. There are different approaches to accomplishing all of these goals, and out of them, I find the Zettelkasten method adapted to space learning to be the best overall. And I tend to keep it in Notion as there are a lot of other knowledge databases I have. Here is the template [5] based on my setup with a couple of examples you can copy. It looks something like in Figure 16-1.

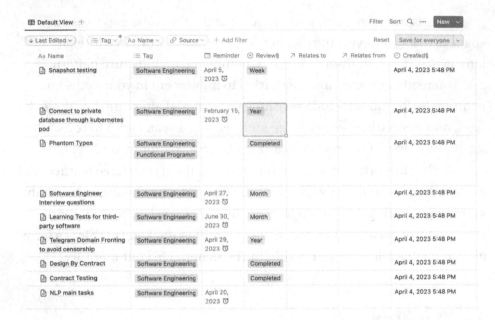

Figure 16-1. *Zettelkasten Notion template*

In brief, the idea of Zettelkasten consists of the following points:

- Write material with your own words (it also enhances remembering).

- Link related ideas to find connections (Linked to, Linked from columns).

- Stick to atomicity, one note should correspond to one short idea (I don't always follow it as it is tedious to write five ideas about one specific topic in five notes).

- Set the note for later repetition (using reminder and review column with gaps of one week, one month, one year).

Another cool technique to take notes if you are more of a visual learner is mind maps. It is fairly useful when you try to connect ideas that lie in a similar area like when you are trying to learn functional programming, for example. You draw bigger topics like first-class function, no side effects, and lazy evaluations and branch them out to go into more specifics.

Find Some Peers

Learning in a group is a good way to enhance productivity [6]. It can help with multiple things simultaneously:

- Leverage a social responsibility which is motivating

- Having a group of people who can support you

- Having more fun while doing it with friends

- Having people around you, you can ask questions

- Having people you can recite what you have learned and exchange opinions

Studying in a group is a typical companion of joining a university, formal courses, or even short online courses, and I find it pretty valuable because it can be a little more challenging to find a group to learn with outside of these options. However, you can try to create a learning group at work so that you learn chosen areas or specific topics with colleagues and share what you have learned in knowledge-sharing sessions with others regularly.

I've seen a very cool idea of having a learning group in a company for functional languages, security, databases, and optimization. Each consisted of two to five people, and they gathered every week for an hour to discuss what they had learned on the topic. And once per half a year, the company would have a big internal presentation where each group does a presentation on the hottest or the most interesting topic they had learned.

Commitment

Setting deadlines for yourself or making a commitment to a friend that you'll finish studying a certain topic by a particular date can really increase your motivation. This is a strategy that's effectively used by courses and universities. Without being accountable to anyone, it's much easier to abandon the learning process, especially if it's a broad and complex subject.

What I often do are artificial deadlines by deciding when I will complete a task. Alternatively, I make a commitment to my wife that I'll finish studying a certain subject or reading a particular book by a certain date. Even though there are no tangible consequences if I miss the deadline, it still provides an extra layer of motivation because it makes the goal feel more significant.

Summary

Learning is a never-ending process for software engineers, so we need to do it right. I use the following techniques that make my learning more effective:

- Dedicated time slots for learning in the calendar

- Touching things with my programming hands as much as possible

- Revisiting material I learn using spaced learning and retelling to others

- Taking notes using Notion + Zettelkasten + spaced learning

- Having a group to learn with

- Set a deadline or a commitment to somebody

References

[1]   www.nature.com/articles/s41586-020-2870-z.epdf

[2]   www.pnas.org/doi/10.1073/pnas.1821936116

[3]   www.apa.org/science/about/psa/2016/06/
       learning-memory

[4]   www.sciencedirect.com/topics/agricultural-and-
       biological-sciences/forgetting-curve

[5]   https://glowing-quill-982.notion.site/d7e
       0e116095c4320a79e3065b5b10405?v=dd2aa46ffbf349a
       9b3c8c0484634b49b

[6]   www.oxfordlearning.com/studying-alone-vs-
       studying-in-a-group/

CHAPTER 17

Feedback

Navigating the software engineering field can be tough. It's important to constantly check if what you're doing is right. Self-reflection is helpful, but it's easy to overlook something from your own point of view. That's why I rely heavily on giving and receiving feedback. Feedback is great for learning, and research shows it significantly boosts learning outcomes [1]. And having a culture where everyone gives and gets feedback helps the team as it builds trust and reminds us we're all here to learn.

How to Get Feedback

Feedback from your colleagues is a very powerful tool. It's the best way to find out if your actions are on track. However, many won't voice their opinions or suggest improvements unless you explicitly ask them. So, it's beneficial to seek feedback, especially when working on tasks where others might have more expertise. Generally, I ask for feedback in these contexts:

- **Public Speeches**: After giving a speech, I select a few audience members and ask for their feedback—what they liked, what they didn't, and suggestions for improvement.

- **Architecture Documents**: I approach experienced software engineers or software architects in my company for a review.

© Mykyta Chernenko 2023
M. Chernenko, *The Rational Software Engineer*,
https://doi.org/10.1007/978-1-4842-9795-7_17

- **Team Collaboration**: When interacting with my or other teams or a new department, I inquire if they see areas for improvement in our collaboration or communication.

- **Mentoring**: After sessions, I ask mentees about their experience and if there's anything they'd want differently.

- **Decision-Making**: For major decisions, from strategic aspects to specific coding tasks, I engage others. They often have unique perspectives and ideas that I haven't thought of.

- **Code Reviews**: When I write a significant piece of code, I seek feedback to ensure it's up to standard and get others' opinions.

- **Incident Reviews**: After resolving an incident, I discuss my approach with others to find potential improvements.

- **Pair Programming**: During these sessions, I ask my coding partner for any suggestions to better my coding process.

One more point on feedback: I always aim to demonstrate, through my actions and words, that I welcome any feedback. Even if someone notices the smallest area for improvement, I encourage them to share it with me. And when somebody gives me feedback, I'm trying to express my gratitude for that. This approach has made a significant difference. When I make my openness to feedback clear by stating it out loud, people feel easier to approach me with their insights and do it more often.

Some feedback will be hard to hear and some may be even nonconstructive because not everybody knows how to do it right. My general rule is to take it all and filter what I don't need out because I feel that I get much more feedback this way in comparison to if I asked people to only give me constructive feedback and only when I ask them for it. It creates an image in general that they need to be careful with me and that the feedback must be given in a very ethical manner if at all. This is great, but it takes so much effort that most people would just avoid giving feedback after such words because it's both easier and safer not to, which is why I try to show that I'm willing to take it all.

However, if you notice that feedback from a person brings you more bad than good, it may be worth simply stopping asking for feedback from the person.

Anonymous Feedback

Sometimes you will feel that people are still reluctant to openly share what they think and give you some sort of feedback; while there can be many underlying reasons you can address, one of them can be that some people are simply scared to do so, especially if a setting includes a lot of other people or giving feedback can hurt their reputation in some way.

One of the good ways to collect feedback in this case is to provide an option to give anonymous feedback through some platforms. It can be as simple as creating a Google Form that you share. In some settings, it's the only way to let people feel more relaxed about what they can say and when.

Feedback Processes

Feedback is much more effective if it is part of the routine that exists in your team or your company. If you can integrate feedback into a process, it will create a feedback-giving culture and will regularly create some insights. Here are a few team processes that can spark an effective feedback culture:

- **Stand-Up Feedback**: Dedicate some minutes at the end of every stand-up to give people time to share their feedback about various things.

- **Colleagues 360 Feedback**: Incorporate giving feedback to your teammates during 360 feedback.

- **Retrospectives**: Retrospectives and postmortems can also be good events to dedicate some time for feedback as feedback is very useful in avoiding future bugs and improving the dynamic in the team in general.

- **Anonymous Feedback Box**: The idea I described above in the context of a team. Every member can write a note there anonymously, and when you have a decent amount of them, you can address them at a dedicated meeting.

How to Give Feedback

I always try to provide constructive feedback to others as well. At the same time, people can have very different reactions to receiving feedback. Some can feel easily criticized for receiving feedback even if it is given in a very constructive and supportive manner. So the first rule that is sometimes missed from the guidelines that I cannot stress more is **to ask the person if the feedback would like the feedback at all.** I try to not jump straight ahead with providing my "precious" opinion because some people are just fine without it. But there are sure situations where you need to provide feedback anyway, like in a case when a person offends other teammates, disrupts team spirit, or doesn't meet the performance expectations. The main rules for providing good feedback are the following:

- State why you give the feedback and what you want to accomplish.

- Describe your feelings and how you see the situation if it's needed. It's a good approach, especially if you provide negative feedback and expect the person to change. For example, saying that the person makes you feel as if your opinion doesn't matter during the meetings because you see that the person gets irritated each time you propose an idea is a good start of feedback as it focuses on how you feel and you don't blame the person for anything.

- Don't focus on personality, focus on the action. We tend to generalize a person's bad behavior to the person's personality and attack it instead. It's not the right attitude. All of us act irresponsibly from time to time, but not all of us become irresponsible in general because of that.

- Give a recommendation on how to improve the situation if appropriate.

- Discuss the person's opinion on the situation, their feeling, and next steps.

Summary

- External feedback uncovers blind spots that self-reflection misses.

- A feedback-rich culture promotes trust and learning in a team.

- Actively request feedback in areas like public talks, document reviews, collaboration, mentoring, and coding.

- Foster an environment around you that encourages all feedback types.

- Prioritize giving and receiving constructive feedback.

- When giving feedback, be clear, focus on actions (not personalities), and ensure it's a two-way conversation.

- Provide a way to give anonymous feedback.

- Incorporate feedback-sparking team processes.

Reference

[1]   https://educationendowmentfoundation.org.uk/
       education-evidence/teaching-learning-toolkit/
       feedback

CHAPTER 18

Learning from Other People

People around us are an endless source of learning. There's almost always something useful that someone else knows that you don't. There are also various strategies and situations that help maximize learning from others. Let's dive into them.

Be the Worst in the Group

Learning from others often means surrounding yourself with people from whom you can gain the most knowledge. For software engineers, it suggests being in a team with high expertise. If you're a software engineer with a few years of experience, you'll easily find teams that have members with far more experience than you do, offering rich learning opportunities. Even for those more advanced in their careers, one cannot know it all, meaning that while one individual might bring less new information on average, there's always valuable information to learn from the teammates.

It's particularly beneficial if many team members have more experience than you. That's why I see value in being part of a team where I might be the worst. The potential for learning becomes huge. And even if you've been a standout software engineer for a decade and you feel that there is less and less what fellow programmers can teach you, focusing on teammates with other specializations has a lot to offer. Pairing with a

© Mykyta Chernenko 2023
M. Chernenko, *The Rational Software Engineer*,
https://doi.org/10.1007/978-1-4842-9795-7_18

senior AQA, for instance, can introduce you to testing approaches and mindsets you didn't think thoroughly about. Likewise, collaborating with a security expert or DevOps can help you understand their best practices and tools.

This idea leads me to try to participate in sessions where experts share their skills as this most often involves completely different skills from mine and brings a lot of education. For instance, if you're keen on understanding product management better, joining a product manager on a user interview can offer invaluable insights

Mentoring

Mentoring is useful for everyone, regardless of experience level. Having someone guide and teach you is often invaluable. The great thing is that at work, you can often find mentors willing to help at no cost. So, it's wise to make the most of this opportunity.

How to Choose a Mentor?

Mentoring is a dynamic process, and as you rapidly grow and acquire new knowledge, the mentor you need will quickly change as well.

Ideally, your mentor should align with the exact experience you aim to achieve. Are you a junior? A mid-level professional might be your best mentor. Seeking management skills? Connect with someone with management responsibilities. It's easy to aim too high, which can backfire. For instance, if you're at a mid-level and you get a CTO managing 400 people as your mentor, they are unlikely to offer the specific guidance you need. They reached your level many years ago, making it harder to relate to your current challenges. Someone who was at a mid-level just a couple of years before will be a much better fit.

Also, consider someone who inspires you, someone you can see as a role model, even on a smaller scale. If a senior engineer doesn't embody the qualities you hope to embrace, why choose them as your mentor? Pick a mentor who exemplifies the expertise and behavior you aspire to.

For those with considerable experience, it might be useful to select a mentor from a domain vastly different from yours. I recently needed to choose a mentor, our CTO was my manager, so it was a no-brainer to ask him. But giving it a thorough thinking, I recognized that our CEO possessed more diverse knowledge that would be more enlightening for me and much further from what I already know. So I approached our CEO for mentorship, believing it would offer a richer educational experience. Eventually, it turned out to be a very good choice as he had a very different perspective and background from mine, which resulted in tons of useful advice and insights.

Lastly, ensure your mentor can effectively communicate and teach. While it may be challenging to determine initially, some individuals naturally convey concepts clearer than others. A mentor's vast work experience won't help if they can't share it well. Aim for someone with a positive mentoring track record or, at the very least, for someone who shows skills for clear explanations and a willingness to teach others.

Where to Find a Mentor?

Your organization is a great starting point for mentorship. Many companies have official mentoring programs. If not, it's still possible to identify someone whose knowledge you value and ask them directly. While some hesitate to make such requests, in a professional setting, I've always received positive responses when asking for mentorship. It's likely you will too.

If your organization lacks the mentoring setup or doesn't have someone with the experience you're seeking, other options are available. Consider seeking external mentors. Numerous platforms exist for this, offering both pro bono and paid mentorship opportunities.

The last approach is "unofficial" mentoring. This involves learning from individuals without formally establishing a mentor-mentee relationship. First, identify those with some bits of experience you want to learn, or simply excellent software engineers, and observe their practices. Engaging them with questions about specific topics and working with them closely daily can be as much enlightening as establishing a format mentorship.

How to Have a Mentoring Session?

Mentoring sessions don't necessarily require a rigid format. However, it's essential to come prepared with specific topics or areas you wish to learn about and develop. Remember, the mentor's role is to aid your growth, so clarity in your objectives helps them provide the guidance you need. Always bring a list of topics, and write down critical takeaways for future reference. Even if you can't make notes in real time, like if your session is during a lunch meeting, make sure to record your insights later to avoid forgetting them.

The structure and duration of mentoring aren't set in stone. It doesn't have to be a fixed hour every week for a year. Some expertise might only require a few sessions. For instance, if you aim to learn about handling big data from sensors based on someone's past experiences, it could take just a few meetings for them to share their insights. So, instead of committing to a year-long process, it might only span five sessions over a month.

Pair Programming

Pair programming is not just about improving code quality or reducing bugs—it's a powerful learning tool. Observing another coder in action offers insights into their preferred tools, development, and debugging setups, and unique techniques for tackling specific coding challenges.

By coding collaboratively, you can pick up new strategies and optimize your own processes. It's an opportunity to continuously learn from one another if you engage in pair programming sessions with your teammates.

Learning by Others' Mistakes

Mistakes are inevitable throughout our careers, and they offer valuable learning opportunities. Each time you make a mistake, there's a lesson to be learned. However, it can be even more beneficial to learn from the mistakes of others, thus avoiding those errors yourself in the future. This is why retrospectives are crucial, as well as simply asking others about their recent missteps. Not all failures are visible to everyone, so these conversations can reveal a lot of details you can learn from.

Whenever someone else makes a mistake, I see it as an opportunity to learn and avoid repeating the same error. It's knowledge gained the hard way, and it's incredibly valuable.

Along the same lines, it is important to give others a chance to learn from your mistakes. So be open when something goes wrong and present the education you got out of it so that others don't do the same. It makes sense to prepare an internal talk or to write a blog post on the topic if it is something bigger and write on a chat if it is a smaller thing.

Paying Tribute

Lastly, and very importantly, as you absorb a lot from others, it's crucial to give back to maintain balance. Some individuals will dedicate hours to mentor you, while others may unknowingly contribute significantly to your learning by serving as role models or unofficial mentors. They all deserve acknowledgment and appreciation. This can be as simple as saying "thanks" when you learn from someone. If their insights have been particularly beneficial, be even more generous in your words and actions; they need to know that you value it.

Similarly, your knowledge could be a treasure to others, so consider mentoring others at all stages of your career. Even if you've just started your first job, there will be people who are learning and trying to secure their first job. There's always someone who will benefit from your mentoring, and it also helps the software engineering community at large.

Summary

- **Recognize Everyone as a Learning Source**: Everyone has unique insights and knowledge to share.

- **Be the Least Experienced in a Group**: Joining a team with higher expertise accelerates learning.

- **Engage in Mentoring**: It's a valuable resource across all career stages.

- **Choosing a Mentor**: Match with someone who aligns with your immediate goals.

- **Finding a Mentor**: Start by looking within your organization.

- **Effective Mentoring Sessions**: Come prepared with specific learning topics.

- **Pair Programming**: It offers mutual learning through coding collaboration.

- **Learn from Others' Mistakes**: Seek insights from colleagues' experiences to avoid repeating errors.

- **Pay Forward and Recognize Others' Efforts**: Give back and appreciate the learning you receive.

CHAPTER 19

Sharing Your Knowledge

Sharing your knowledge is beneficial for others and also a powerful technique to enhance your own learning. Firstly, when you explain concepts to others, you structure them consistently and connect various pieces of knowledge you possess [1]. Secondly, this process can highlight knowledge gaps, especially if you're uncertain or questioned about topics you're not familiar with. Lastly, sharing information boosts retention, similar to the effect of reciting. Let's talk more about the best ways to share your knowledge.

Yourself

It might seem odd, but attempting to explain a concept to yourself or a rubber duck is incredibly beneficial. This exercise prompts you to consider the topic thoroughly, just as if you were explaining it to someone else. Plus, it's the most judgment-free method; you're your own audience, so there's no fear of criticism if you forget or don't know something. Sometimes, after learning something new, I'll take a moment to internally articulate it, as if I described it to another individual.

© Mykyta Chernenko 2023
M. Chernenko, *The Rational Software Engineer*,
https://doi.org/10.1007/978-1-4842-9795-7_19

Friends and Team

The simplest way to share knowledge is to immediately discuss it with someone who might find it intriguing. For instance, if I come across an interesting software topic, I often chat about it with a colleague or friend who shares the same interests. Regular discussions during coffee breaks or lunch with my team about new technologies or valuable insights are common for me.

While this method requires minimal preparation and I tend to use it frequently, it's crucial to be mindful of not overwhelming others. To prevent this, I diversify whom I share with, ensuring I don't frequently talk about my learning topics with the same person. This way, I avoid bothering them.

In Company

You can still spread your knowledge to a broader audience without much preparation. I often post a quick message on the company-wide tech chat with something I've found interesting and useful for our daily work, which allows me to both recap and help others with their task and problems.

On the other hand, there are options that require more planning. They can seem time-consuming, but they are actually incredibly beneficial for learning, as you'll need to structure the knowledge you've acquired in a clear, comprehensible way. I particularly enjoy hosting brown-bag sessions during lunch. These sessions are usually laid-back, so there's no pressure to deliver a top-tier presentation. Still, you reap all the usual benefits. Plus, such initiatives increase your visibility and display your passion, encouraging others to share their knowledge or, at the very least, leave a positive impression of you.

Conferences

Attending and presenting at conferences require a substantial amount of preparation and effort, but the advantages are even greater. Normally, you can't just present what you already know; you'll need to delve deeper and learn more in order to generate enough material for a 30-minute presentation. This encourages you to understand subjects in depth and develop expertise. It functions as both a motivational deadline and a tool for structuring your knowledge. Moreover, it means you'll get to experiment with visual elements, exploring effective ways to convey information visually. This skill comes in handy when explaining concepts to your team or during an architecture review as visual aids can clarify many details and offer a succinct overview.

Additionally, this can increase your visibility if you're presenting at an internal conference in your company, a common occurrence in medium to large-sized firms. Alternatively, if you're speaking at a public conference, it can help you build connections and meet like-minded individuals. It's common for attendees to approach speakers before or after their talk, often leading to valuable connections. Plus, having public speaking experience is an attractive addition to your CV.

Articles

Writing articles has similarities with presenting at conferences in that it often requires deep dives into subjects to articulate them effectively. However, articles introduce new advantages. For one, the potential reach of an article can be vast. A well-written piece on a popular platform can easily be read and found beneficial by thousands.

When you learn extensively or deal with intricate subjects at work, it can be beneficial to start a personal tech blog. Here, you can methodically break down and articulate your learnings in a series of consistent articles.

While this is a significant time investment, the rewards are great as well. It enhances your written communication skills, potentially helps a broader audience with valuable insights, and serves as an impressive addition to your CV.

Mentoring

Mentoring offers a unique opportunity to share both recent knowledge and lessons learned in the past. What's particularly beneficial is that sometimes you'll get asked questions on subjects that you once mastered but have become a bit rusty on since. This challenge allows you to revisit and refresh your understanding. As you explain, you're also reinforcing the knowledge for yourself. If needed, you can review the topic and then explain it better at the next session. Additionally, I appreciate when mentees share topics they wish to cover in advance. It gives me the chance to refresh my memory and structure the explanation optimally.

Social Platforms

We've covered before that social presence helps in a lot of aspects of the career. So you can reap even more benefits from sharing your knowledge on various social platforms. It will both make you visible, can expand your social circle, and will teach you how to drastically adapt your content to the medium you use. For example, if you are to share something on Twitter, YouTube, and LinkedIn, there will be three very distinct styles in which you will share the material.

Summary

- **Structured Learning**: Explaining concepts helps in interconnecting your knowledge and identifying gaps.

- **Self-Articulation**: Reinforce understanding by explaining topics to yourself, offering a judgment-free environment.

- **Casual Sharing**: Discuss recent learnings with friends or colleagues but avoid overwhelming the same person.

- **In-Company Sharing**: Post updates or host informal sessions. Increases visibility and encourages mutual learning.

- **Conferences**: Dive deep into subjects and present; aid in networking and boost resume value.

- **Writing**: Articles and blogs expand your reach, refine communication skills, and can assist many.

- **Mentoring**: Revisit old concepts, strengthen understanding, and structure information effectively through teaching.

- **Social Platforms**: Share knowledge on social platforms to both boost your social presence and gain the same benefits.

Reference

[1]   www.livescience.com/34000-explaining-helps-understand.htm

CHAPTER 20

Learning from Code

As a software engineer, one of the most valuable resources for learning is the code itself. It becomes particularly beneficial if the code base you work with is new at least every six months. This ensures you don't become too rooted in one method of coding, a trap that's easy to avoid if you're rotating to a different team within a company regularly or if you're a consultant.

The real beauty of code lies in its practicality. Beyond just theoretical debates or architectural patterns, code is tangible and functional. It clearly demonstrates that many isolated patterns might not be as effective or might address only a part of the challenge. A well-written, extensive code base helps one discover unique techniques and hands-on solutions that aren't typically discussed in books or presented at conferences. To fully benefit from this learning, it's essential to understand how to maximize the lessons drawn from code. Let's begin this exploration by exploring the crucial aspect of quickly familiarizing oneself with the new code base when joining a new project.

Onboarding on a Project Quickly

Understanding code is the first step to learning from it, and it's beneficial to get this understanding quickly. This not only aids in learning but also enables you to make meaningful decisions about the project. I've often observed an approach where people focus solely on one part of a project, not bothering to understand how everything else connects together.

© Mykyta Chernenko 2023
M. Chernenko, *The Rational Software Engineer*,
https://doi.org/10.1007/978-1-4842-9795-7_20

While being mainly responsible for one part of the code isn't a negative—
it typically means you can efficiently improve the functionality you're
familiar with—it does limit the potential learning you can derive from the
code and restricts your comprehension of the project as a whole.

When I join a project, I usually ask for at least a week without extensive
tasks, giving me time to comprehend as much as possible about the
project.

Teammates and Documentation

The initial crucial step to understanding a project quickly is to
communicate with those already involved in the project. Firstly, it's
important to get an overall picture of the project, providing a foundation
for your mental model. Secondly, you should ask for the most recent
documentation about the project as it's often a structured and easy-to-get
resource for further learning.

Once you've acquired the most recent documentation, it's essential to
read through it entirely. While it might be tempting to skip this step and
dive into understanding the code directly, the documentation can be a
huge time-saver. Not only does it provide a broader view, like architectural
diagrams, but it also offers insight into the rationale behind certain
decisions.

There have been instances when I've questioned specific choices in
a project, only to realize the reasoning behind them after consulting the
documentation or the pull requests made by the code's authors. Often, I
might believe a different technology would be better suited for a task in
a project, but after reading through evaluations of various technologies
and the team's final choice, the decision becomes clearer. For example,
when I was onboarded on one project, it had a pipeline of tasks, which
we triggered by a self-written queue-like solution in Postgres. It was
very simple but lacked a lot of functionality in terms of observability
and scalability. Knowing that a queue system would be more suitable

according to the common architecture patterns, I started evaluating RabbitMQ, ZeroMQ, Redis, and other solutions. But after all of the considerations, I came to a conclusion that the simple effort to deploy the new technology would be greater than improving the existing solution. What is funnier in that situation is that not only did I spend time to come to the same conclusion that the authors of the project came to but I also found a document later on where they explained all of their reasoning. The document I could have easily noticed if I had spent more time reading the documentation. After that, I focus on reading through all the relevant documentation first.

Here are the primary areas I focus on in the documentation:

- The overall architecture, including all diagrams.

- The reasoning behind architectural decisions and any alternatives considered.

- The technical stack, especially focusing on any technologies I might need to familiarize myself with further.

- Data structure, databases, and understanding the data flow and processing.

- Recognized limitations or issues in the project, which can help pinpoint potential problem areas.

- Monitoring and observability configurations, guiding me on where to look if bugs arise and to solve them quicker.

- Access to different tools. I ensure to set these up as soon as I get access, so I'm prepared when troubleshooting is required.

- Recommended project setup and essential debugging tools.

- Development processes and coding conventions, which can vary widely between teams. This includes everything from deploying code through CI/CD pipelines to incident handling procedures.

- External dependencies, including other teams and third-party tools.

- Testing approaches.

- Contact details for all individuals relevant to the project, helping me know who to reach out to for specific questions and clarifying individual responsibilities.

- Identifying key stakeholders and understanding their roles.

- User stories, Jobs to Be Done, and other product-related documents, providing context on the project's purpose.

- Current objectives, OKRs, and the project road map to grasp the future direction.

If comprehensive documentation isn't available, your teammates often become the go-to resource. Seek them out and request a walk-through of the project. They can shed light on the primary components, how these elements interconnect, and the rationale behind key decisions made throughout the project's development. To benefit future team members, it's wise to record this walk-through. This way, it can be shared with individuals who join after you. Additionally, having an automatic transcript of the conversation can be a handy reference, allowing you to revisit specific points at your leisure.

Project Code

After gaining insights from your teammates, dive into the project code yourself. Your goal is to piece together a mental map of how the primary components function. The depth of your understanding will largely depend on the project's size. In some cases, you might grasp all the pivotal concepts and code segments. In other instances, especially with larger code bases, you may only get a general sense of the areas you'll be directly involved with. Regardless, when you go through the code, try to go into the sequence of function calls until you've constructed a clear overarching picture. It's usually unnecessary to go into the implementation of every abstraction if you have a clear understanding of what the abstraction means. For instance, if there's a function that retrieves a user from a database using an ID, you can generally stop there without diving deep into the specifics of user retrieval. The goal is to craft a foundational understanding that you can build on top of.

Lastly, consider incorporating pair programming sessions into your onboarding process. The benefits of this method are substantial. Many companies even embed this technique into their onboarding protocols, encouraging new members to participate in five to ten pair programming sessions during their initial weeks. As seasoned members of the team, we take some things for granted or forget to explain something to the newcomers. During a walk-through, it's easy to miss out on explaining some aspects, thinking they're either too obvious or simply forgetting they need clarification. However, when a newcomer joins in coding, they tap into this reservoir of "implicit knowledge." The interactive nature of pair programming allows for immediate questions and answers, fostering a deep and rapid understanding. Despite its evident advantages, it's surprising how underutilized this technique remains during onboarding in general.

Further Learning

After onboarding to a project, it doesn't necessarily mean you fully understand every aspect of it. Particularly with active projects, as you develop certain segments, the code base is simultaneously evolving in other areas due to contributions from teammates. This ongoing development requires continuous learning on your part.

Deeper immersion into the project will be necessary after initial onboarding. Expanding your understanding and developing a comprehensive mind map of the project is vital for making informed decisions. This deep dive can be achieved by independently exploring the remaining code, talking with colleagues responsible for different project parts, or taking on tasks outside your usual area of responsibility on the project. If you find yourself repeatedly working on the same aspect or becoming the gatekeeper in a specific area, consider asking for different tasks that will widen your knowledge about the project.

Once you've achieved a broad understanding of the project (or at least a significant portion of it), sharing this knowledge with other teams is a nice thing to do. A recommended approach is to start creating a presentation during your onboarding phase, noting key topics you plan to cover. As you progress, continue to populate this presentation with new insights. This not only serves as a personal learning tool guide but also helps identify areas you're less familiar with.

Given the effort involved in creating such presentations, it's not uncommon that teams rarely share such presentations with other teams. But for you, it's much less of an effort as you are learning and going through the whole project to familiarize yourself with it anyway. Sharing knowledge in this way not only solidifies your understanding but also enriches the broader company knowledge base.

Lastly, make it a habit to keep an eye on all the key pull requests (PRs) being submitted even if you are not requested to review them. When PRs come with detailed descriptions, you might not need to go into the code to grasp the key changes. But, if the volume of PRs is manageable, thoroughly reviewing them from start to finish and offering insightful feedback is always beneficial.

Summary

Code base Is Essential for Learning:

- **Diverse Code Bases**: Regularly rotating to new code bases prevents stagnation and promotes continuous learning.

- **Tangible Learning**: Actual code provides hands-on solutions, often revealing insights not found in theoretical resources.

Onboarding Quickly:

- **Collaborate with Team**: Gather foundational knowledge from current team members.

- **Document Deep Dive**: Thoroughly review project documentation to understand architecture, technical stack, data flow, tools, team members, and project goals.

- **Code Walk-through**: Seek insights from team members and mentally map main components.

- **Pair Programming**: Engage in sessions during the initial weeks for hands-on, interactive learning.

Continuous Learning:

- **Deep Dive**: Post-onboarding, further immerse yourself in the project and regularly update your understanding.

- **Knowledge Sharing**: As you understand more, consider sharing insights with other teams through presentations or documentation.

- **Monitor Pull Requests**: Keep an eye on all PRs to stay updated, and provide valuable feedback when possible.

CHAPTER 21

Rotation

Long-term focus on a single project or specific area of code can hinder your career progress as a software engineer. Despite potentially gaining considerable expertise in your area of responsibility, your broader knowledge may become limited. Fresh challenges and ideas are vital for continued learning, motivation, and professional growth. The remedy for this stagnation is regular rotation, meaning that you are rotated on a new code base. Although frequently changing code responsibilities or projects might seem counterproductive, I would argue that the benefits of rotation outweigh the drawbacks. Let's discuss the advantages and disadvantages and explore effective strategies for rotation.

In-Project Rotation

A rotation within your current project can often be the easiest move as it allows you to maintain team dynamics and knowledge continuity while slightly adjusting your focus. The main reason for doing this, beyond self-improvement and learning as a software engineer, is to prevent the formation of silos.

Silos can easily emerge in a project when team members are assigned rigid roles and their responsibilities are split among different areas of the codebase. Imagine a team consisting of a dedicated AQA, DevOps, front-end developer, and several back-end developers, each having their

© Mykyta Chernenko 2023
M. Chernenko, *The Rational Software Engineer*,
https://doi.org/10.1007/978-1-4842-9795-7_21

own project module to look after. While such a setup might initially seem advantageous, with everyone working on what they're best at, it can lead to a bunch of problems.

One significant issue that arises from this arrangement is the lack of versatile perspectives. When you're the sole developer of a module or a particular code area, everyone expects you to have the best understanding of it. Even in the presence of a formal PR review process from other teammates, most people won't question decisions or fully comprehend the implications of code written in someone else's module. Consequently, this situation can decrease the benefits traditionally derived from code reviews. If knowledge silos and rigid roles characterize a project, it means that all decisions are essentially backed by just a single opinion.

Another problem is the low bus factor coupled with a high turnover rate, which is unfortunately typical in the software engineering field. The term "bus factor" refers to the vulnerability of a project if a few critical team members suddenly become unavailable. Picture this: your DevOps and AQA, who are the only ones familiar with and able to maintain the solutions they created, decide to leave for a better job opportunity. The following week, your team is tasked with releasing a new microservice. This release entails significant changes to testing and demands additional deployment configurations. With those key players gone, no one truly comprehends how things worked before, leaving the team without the necessary expertise. This terrible scenario is not uncommon in many projects.

Raising the bus factor becomes crucial. One strategy to achieve this is ensuring that team members' responsibilities intersect. For instance, one software engineer could regularly collaborate with the AQA, cowriting tests, while another might focus on the DevOps domain. While this is a step in the right direction, I believe an even more comprehensive approach is needed. Everyone should possess the capability to navigate each other's technical areas on the project. This doesn't imply that all members will become experts in every facet, like DevOps or front end, but they should at least comprehend how the code works, be competent in making modifications, and have periodic tasks within the domains where they can get hands-on experience.

Fortunately, the benefits of rotation are usually evident to tech leads and management as they're often familiar with the challenges mentioned. The main obstacle arises when some software engineers are hesitant about taking on additional responsibilities or rotating roles, given the significant cognitive load involved. While I don't think it is necessary to push these individuals too hard, they should be encouraged to take other aspects with relevant asks here and there. Meanwhile, those who are more eager to broaden their skill will take more active roles in promoting rotation and fostering positive team dynamics.

In-Company Rotation

Switching to a different project offers a wealth of fresh insights, given the new codebase, new colleagues, and novel concepts. This kind of rotation can be equated to changing companies in terms of the learning and career advancements it provides.

One clear advantage is the influx of new perspectives. Every new team member, having come from a different background, views problems through a unique lens, offering a fresh take on solutions. They can highlight potential weaknesses or flaws in current approaches that might have been overlooked by those deeply ingrained in the project. Additionally, given their familiarity with other projects within the same organization, they're better positioned to collaborate effectively with prior teams.

However, such rotational strategies aren't as widely embraced as one might expect. The practice of frequently transitioning between projects isn't as common, making it harder to advocate for. If your management fails to recognize the value in such rotation, it's essential to emphasize its importance, not only for your personal motivation but also for your career trajectory.

With the pros covered, let's now cover the potential drawbacks and inappropriate timings for initiating rotation.

Cons

One significant drawback of rotation is the time it consumes. You can't just dive into a new project and expect peak efficiency instantly. While minor tasks might not necessitate profound knowledge, fully immersing oneself in a project for an extended period can span days, if not weeks. It's crucial, therefore, to strike a balance—rotate to break knowledge silos and learn, but also ensure consistent productivity.

Moreover, if you're considering rotation as a short-term solution to boost project manpower, think again. Imagine you're trying to meet a feature deadline in the upcoming week but are lagging. In such scenarios, introducing a new member might be more detrimental than beneficial. The onboarding process not only requires time but also diverts the attention of existing team members who have to assist the newcomer.

Lastly, frequent rotations can obstruct the development of profound expertise. By constantly switching tasks or roles, one might find it challenging to acquire an in-depth understanding of complex concepts. For instance, in situations where every hour of downtime could cost millions, it's crucial for both DevOps and software engineers to diagnose and resolve production issues rapidly. This proficiency often arises from deep familiarity with a system, which could be compromised if rotations are too frequent.

Thus, I advise against switching between projects more frequently than once every three to six months. Similarly, when exploring a new domain within an existing project, I'd recommend doing so no more than once a month.

Summary

- Rotation prevents knowledge silos, promotes growth, and boosts project resilience.

- In-project rotation keeps team dynamics while diversifying code focus.

- In-company rotation offers fresh perspectives, akin to changing companies.

- Drawbacks: Time-consuming, potentially detrimental near deadlines, may hinder deep expertise.

- Recommended frequency: In-company every three to six months, in-project once a month.

Index

A

Acceptance and commitment
therapy (ACT), 33
Aristotle, 11
Atomic Habits, 34, 38

B

Burnout, 2
  causes
    distress, 72
    goals/targets, 68
    high workload, 65–67
    inefficient processes, 67
    lack of change, 70
    lack of community, 69, 70
    lack of control, 71
    lack of values, 71
    play, 74
    recovery, 73
  primary signs, 63
  red flags
    passive and cynical, 65
    play, 65
    vacation, 64
  software engineers, 64

C

Calendar and time booking
system, 9
Career change, 3
  feeling stuck, 87
  SMART goals, 85–87
  software engineer
    big changes, 89
    Ikigai, 88
    machine learning, 93
    management, 90
    tools, 92
    T-shaped developers, 92
  switch fields, 94
ChatGPT, 7, 102, 113, 165
Code base
  deep-dive, 214
  knowledge sharing, 214
  learning, 213
  project
    code, 211
    teammates/
    documentation, 208–210
  PRs, 213, 214
  teammates, 212
  techniques, 207

© Mykyta Chernenko 2023
M. Chernenko, *The Rational Software Engineer*,
https://doi.org/10.1007/978-1-4842-9795-7

Printed in the United States
by Baker & Taylor Publisher Services